Exploring maths

Home Book

7

PEARSON

Longman

Anita Straker, Tony Fisher, Rosalyn Hyde, Sue Jennings and Jonathan Longstaffe

Published and distributed by Pearson Education Limited, Edinburgh Gate, Harlow, Essex, CM20 2JE, England

www.pearsonschoolsandfecolleges.co.uk

First published 2009

ISBN-13 978-1-405-84423-9

Typeset by Tech-Set, Gateshead

Printed and bound in Great Britain at Scotprint, Haddington

The publisher's policy is to use paper manufactured from sustainable forests.

Picture credits

The publisher would like to thank the following for their kind permission to reproduce their photographs:

(Key: b-bottom; c-centre; l-left; r-right; t-top)

Alamy Images: Ron Buskirk 67; FogStock 109l; Andrew Fox 104; Paul Andrew Lawrence 28t; **Corbis:** Gabe Palmer 109r; **DK Images:** Steve Gorton 94; Paul Harris 23; Kim Sayer 27; **iStockphoto:** 40, 46, 59, 65, 66, 75, 81b, 93; Adrian Beesley 35; Silvia Boratti 44; Peter Eckhardt 28b; Simon Edwin 106; Joe Gough 5; Joanne Green 1; Richard Hobson 115; Darren Hubley 109c; Mojca Kobal 43; David Lewis 11; Stacey Newman 78; Andrea Pelletier 61; Achim Prill 41; Giovanni Rinaldi 71; Steve Rosset 69; Claudio Rossol 70; Jacom Stephens 33; James Thew 111b; Marcelo Wain 124; Amy Walters 22; Trista Weibell 81t; Dan Wood 111t; **Jupiter Unlimited:** Thinkstock Images 10; **Pearson Education Ltd:** Scott Foresman 12; **Jenny Penfold:** 8; **Rex Features:** Denkou Images 116; **Texas Instruments:** Suzie Williams 63, 119

All other images © Pearson Education

Picture Research by: Louise Edgeworth

Acknowledgements

We are grateful to the following for permission to reproduce copyright material:

Data from 'Bolsover Mizuno 10km race 2007'; and 'Great Langdale Christmas Pudding 10km race 2007', granted by kind permission of Athletics Data Ltd, www.thepowerof10.info; Data 'Reaction times of Australian Year 5 Pupils', source: Australian Bureau of Statistics; Data 'Reaction time for Year 5 and 10 pupils in New Zealand' sampled, with permission, from CensusAtSchool New Zealand, www.censusatschool.org.nz; Data from 'Maximum daily temperature in Fort Nelson in Canada for 90 days summer 2007' and 'Max and min daily temperature Fort Nelson in Canada through 2007' copyright © Her Majesty The Queen in Right of Canada, Environment Canada, 2007; Screenshots 'Frieze patterns in cast iron' by Heather McLeay and 'Classifying solids using angle deficiency' by Warwick Evans http://nrich.maths.org, reproduced with permission of NRICH Project; and Data from 'Number of marriages quarterly in England and Wales 2000-2003' National Statistics www.statistics.gov.uk © Crown copyright 2003, Crown Copyright material is reproduced with permission under the terms of the Click-Use License; Edexcel GCSE exam questions granted by kind permission of Edexcel Limited. Edexcel Limited accepts no responsibility whatsoever for the accuracy or method of working in the answers given.

Every effort has been made to trace the copyright holders and we apologise in advance for any unintentional omissions. We would be pleased to insert the appropriate acknowledgement in any subsequent edition of this publication.

Contents

N7.1   Powers and roots   **1**
1   Negative powers   1
2   Fractional indices   2
3   Surds   3

A7.1   Linear graphs and inequalities   **4**
1   Working with coordinates   4
2   Exploring linear graphs   4
3   Simultaneous linear equation   5
4   Linear inequalities in one variable   6
5   Linear inequalities in two variables   7
6   Optimisation problems   8

N7.2   Decimals and accuracy   **9**
1   Significant figures   9
2   Standard form   10
3   Accuracy of measurements   12
4   Upper and lower bounds   13
5   Dimensions   14

S7.1   Enquiry 1   **15**
1   Sampling   15
2   Planning and collecting data   16
3   Drawing histograms   17
4   Choosing class intervals   18
5   Using histograms   19
6   Moving averages   21

G7.1   Measures and mensuration   **23**
1   Arcs and sectors of circles   23
2   Circle problems   25
3   Volume of 3D shapes   26
4   Surface area of 3D shapes   27
5   Problem solving   28

A7.2   Expressions and formulae   **30**
1   Simplifying expressions   30
2   Expanding brackets   31
3   Factorising expressions   32
4   Working with formulae   32
5   Investigations   33
6   Deriving formulae   34

G7.2   Trigonometry 1   **36**
1   Pythagoras' theorem in 3D   36
2   Finding an unknown angle   37
3   Finding an unknown side   38

N7.3   Proportional reasoning   **40**
1   Percentage problems   40
2   Direct proportion 1   41
3   Direct proportion 2   42
4   Inverse proportion   43
5   Proportion and square roots   45

G7.3   Geometrical reasoning   **47**
1   Tangents and chords   47
2   Circle theorems   48
3   More circle theorems   49
4   Using the circle theorems   50
5   Congruent triangles   52
6   Proving congruency   53
7   Similar shapes and solids   54

S7.2   Probability 1   **56**
1   Using tree diagrams   56
2   The probability of combined events   57
3   Investigating a game of chance   59
4   Conditional probability   60
5   The 'and' and 'or' rules   61

A7.3   Solving equations   **62**
1   Linear equations   62
2   Solving quadratic equations graphically   62
3   Solving quadratic equations by factorisation 1   63
4   Solving quadratic equations by factorisation 2   64
5   Completing the square   65
6   Using the quadratic formula   65
7   Simultaneous linear and quadratic equations   66
8   Simultaneous linear and non-linear equations   67

G7.4   Transformations and vectors   **68**
1   Symmetry patterns *(double lesson)*   68
3   Vectors and vector notation   69

4	The magnitude of a vector	70
5	Vector addition	71
6	Parallel vectors and problem solving	72

S7.3   Enquiry 2   **73**
1	Sampling and statistics	73
2	Five-figure summaries	73
3	Cumulative frequency 1	75
4	Cumulative frequency 2	76
5	Estimating statistics for grouped data	77
6	Box plots	78
7	Histograms and frequency density	79
8	Moving averages	80

G7.5   Trigonometry 2   **82**
1	2D and 3D problems	82
2	Area of a triangle	83
3	Angles larger than 90°	84
4	Graphs of trigonometric functions	85
5	The sine rule	86
6	The cosine rule	87
7	Using the sine and cosine rules	89

S7.4   Probability 2   **92**
1	Capture-recapture	92
2	The birthday problem	93
3	Using probability 1	94
4	Using probability 2	95
5	Quincunx	95

A7.4   Exploring graphs   **97**
1	Exploring quadratic and cubic functions	97
2	Properties of polynomial functions	98
3	Reciprocal functions	99
4	Exponential functions	99
5	Generating trigonometric functions	101
6	Exploring trigonometric functions	102
7	Transformations of functions	103
8	Loci	104
9	Solving problems	105

N7.4   Using and applying maths   **106**
1	The history of convex polyhedra (double lesson)	106
3	Algebraic proof	108
4	Careers in mathematics	109

R7.1   Revision unit 1   **110**
1	Percentages and ratios	110
2	Expressions and equations	112
3	Formulae, functions and graphs	113
4	Geometrical reasoning	114
5	Probability	115

R7.2   Revision unit 2   **117**
1	Indices and standard form	117
2	Equations and inequalities	118
3	Functions and graphs	119
4	Pythagoras' theorem and trigonometry	121
5	Graphs, charts and statistics	122

Powers and roots

TASK 1: Negative powers

> **⊙ Points to remember**
>
> ⊙ To **multiply** two numbers in index form, add the indices,
>   so $a^m \times a^n = a^{m+n}$.
> ⊙ To **divide** two numbers in index form, subtract the indices,
>   so $a^m \div a^n = a^{m-n}$.
> ⊙ To **raise a power to a power**, multiply the indices,
>   so $(a^m)^n = a^{m \times n}$.
> ⊙ These rules work for both positive and negative powers.

(1) Simplify these.

    a $3^4 \times 3^{-2}$ **b** $2^{-2} \times 2^{-1}$ **c** $5^{-1} \times 5^{-2}$ **d** $8^{-2} \div 8^{-3}$

    e $5^{-4} \div 5^{-2}$ **f** $10^3 \div 10^{-1}$ **g** $(2^{-2})^3$ **h** $(5^{-4})^{-1}$

(2) Find the value of n in each of these.

    a $3^n = \dfrac{3^3}{3^6}$ **b** $4 \times 4^n = \dfrac{4^3}{4^5}$ **c** $\dfrac{5^n}{5} = \dfrac{5^7}{5^9}$

(3) Which is greater: (4 to the power 3) to the power 2, **or** 4 to the power
(3 to the power 2)?

(4) What is the last digit of 2^{-22}? Explain your answer.

TASK 2: Fractional indices

 Points to remember

- $a^{\frac{1}{2}}$ is the same as the **square root** of a.
- $\sqrt[n]{a}$ or $a^{\frac{1}{n}}$ means the **nth root** of a, e.g. $\sqrt[3]{a}$ or $a^{\frac{1}{3}}$ is the **cube root** of a.
- The **index laws** hold for fractional powers. So:
  $(a^{\frac{1}{m}})^n = a^{\frac{1}{m} \times n} = a^{\frac{n}{m}}$ and $(a^m)^{\frac{1}{n}} = a^{m \times \frac{1}{n}} = a^{\frac{m}{n}}$

1 **Without using a calculator**, work out these values.

     a $16^{\frac{1}{2}}$ **b** $25^{\frac{1}{2}}$ **c** $8^{\frac{1}{3}}$ **d** $1000^{\frac{1}{3}}$

2 **Use a calculator** to work out these values.

     a $625^{\frac{3}{4}}$ **b** $81^{\frac{1}{4}}$ **c** $729^{\frac{5}{6}}$ **d** $3125^{\frac{3}{5}}$

     e $4^{\frac{7}{2}}$ **f** $(-27)^{\frac{2}{3}}$ **g** $(64)^{-\frac{1}{2}}$ **h** $(625)^{-\frac{1}{4}}$

3 Simplify:

     a $z^{\frac{1}{3}} \times z^{\frac{1}{2}}$ **b** $x^{\frac{3}{4}} \div x^{\frac{2}{3}}$

4 A cuboid has a square base.
     Its height is half the length of an edge of the base.

     The volume of the cuboid is 256 cm³. Work out its surface area.

5 Ivana thinks of a two-digit cube number.
     When she swaps over the digits, the number she gets is the product of a cube and a square.
     What number is Ivana thinking of? Explain your answer.

 Did you know that...?

You cannot write the square root of an integer that is not a perfect square as a fraction. It is always an **irrational number**. For example, you cannot write $\sqrt{2}$ as $\frac{a}{b}$, where a and b are integers. However, you can draw $\sqrt{2}$ because it is exactly the length of the diagonal of a square with side length 1.

This has been known since the time of the ancient Greeks.

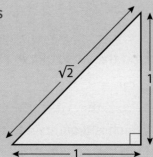

TASK 3: Surds

> ### Points to remember
> ⊙ A **surd** is a root that does not have an exact value.
> ⊙ $\sqrt{a} \times \sqrt{b} = \sqrt{ab}$ and $\dfrac{\sqrt{a}}{\sqrt{b}} = \sqrt{\dfrac{a}{b}}$ and $(\sqrt{a} + \sqrt{b})(\sqrt{a} - \sqrt{b}) = a - b$.
> ⊙ To **rationalise** $\dfrac{a}{\sqrt{b}}$, multiply the numerator and denominator by $\sqrt{b}$.

1 Rationalise the denominators and simplify the answers.

   a $\dfrac{3}{\sqrt{6}}$ **b** $\dfrac{3}{\sqrt{24}}$ **c** $\dfrac{25}{\sqrt{35}}$ **d** $\dfrac{6}{\sqrt{14}}$ **e** $\dfrac{8}{\sqrt{8}}$

2 Work out $\dfrac{(5 + \sqrt{3})(5 - \sqrt{3})}{\sqrt{21}}$. Give your answer in its simplest form.

3 ABCD is a square.
AB is $(1 + \sqrt{3})$ cm.
Show that the area of triangle BCD is $(2 + \sqrt{3})$ cm².

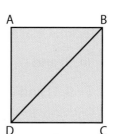

4 Each of the two equal sides in a right-angled triangle is $\dfrac{6}{\sqrt{2}}$ cm.
Find the length of the hypotenuse.

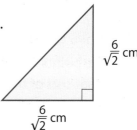

> ### Did you know that...?
> The Greek **Hippasus of Metapontum**, a disciple of **Pythagoras**, is thought to have been the first to prove the existence of $\sqrt{2}$, which he did about 500 BC.
>
> He is thought to have made this discovery while working out the lengths of the sides of a pentagram.
>
> Pythagoras didn't agree with him so, as legend has it, he had Hippasus drowned!

A pentagram

TASK 1: Working with coordinates

● Points to remember

⊙ The length of the line joining (x_1, y_1) and (x_2, y_2) is
$\sqrt{(x_2 - x_1)^2 + (y_2 - y_1)^2}$.

⊙ The midpoint of the line joining (x_1, y_1) and (x_2, y_2) is $\left(\dfrac{x_1 + x_2}{2}, \dfrac{y_1 + y_2}{2}\right)$.

(1) Find the length of the line joining each pair of points. Give your answers to 1 decimal place.

    a (4, 5) and (7, 9)   **b** (1, 1) and (8, 25)   **c** (0, 0) and (9, 12)

    d (−9, 1) and (5, −6)   **e** (−3, −2) and (4, 7)   **f** (−2, −4) and (5, −13)

(2) Find the midpoint of the line joining each pair of points.

    a (4, 6) and (8, 14)   **b** (1, 17) and (16, 2)   **c** (−4, 1) and (10, 5)

    d (−3, 10) and (4, −7)   **e** (−12, −9) and (10, 9)   **f** (−20, −2) and (5, −19)

(3) The points A (4, −2), B (2, 0) and C (6, 2) are joined to form a triangle. What sort of triangle is it?

TASK 2: Exploring linear graphs

● Points to remember

⊙ The graph of $y = ax + b$ has gradient a and intercepts the y-axis at (0, b).

⊙ Parallel lines have the same gradient.

⊙ Any line perpendicular to $y = ax + b$ has gradient $-\dfrac{1}{a}$.

(1) Write the gradient and intercept for the line $y = -7x - 11$ and sketch the graph.

(2) Write the equation of the line parallel to the line $y = 5x - 4$ that passes through (3, 9).

(3) Write the equation of the line perpendicular to the line $y = -3x + 5$ that passes through $(-3, 7)$.

(4) Write the equation of a line that passes through $(-2, -4)$ and $(1, 5)$.

(5) Find the equation of the perpendicular bisector of the line joining $(-3, -4)$ and $(2, 6)$.

TASK 3: Simultaneous linear equations

 Points to remember

⊙ You can use the **method of substitution** to solve simultaneous equations algebraically.

⊙ Alternatively, you can use the **method of elimination** to solve the equations.

⊙ The intersection points of graphs can be used to find simple integer solutions but algebraic methods are needed for non-integer solutions.

(1) Solve these pairs of simultaneous linear equations.

a $7x - 3y = 11$ .... (1)
$5x + 4y = 14$ .... (2)

b $7x + 4y = 29$ .... (1)
$5x - 3y = 9$ .... (2)

c $9x - 2y = 1$ .... (1)
$12x + 3y = 24$ .... (2)

d $13x - 3y = 11$ .... (1)
$9x + 2y = 28$ .... (2)

(2) Solve these pairs of simultaneous linear equations. Give your answers to 1 decimal place.

a $3y - 2x = 21$ .... (1)
$6y + 5x = 9$ .... (2)

b $4x - 5y = 8$ .... (1)
$2x + 3y = -16$ .... (2)

c $2x - 5y = 1$ .... (1)
$3x + 2y = -7$ .... (2)

d $6x - 7y = 3$ .... (1)
$2x + 3y = 10$ .... (2)

(3) Two groups of pigeons live in a tree, one group at the top and the other at the bottom of the tree.

The group at the top say to the others, 'If one of your group joins us our number will be double yours, but if one of our group joins you, your number will be equal to ours.'

How many pigeons are there in each group?

TASK 4: Linear inequalities in one variable

 Points to remember

- You can solve a linear inequality in one variable in much the same way as you solve a linear equation in one variable.
- You can add or subtract a positive or negative number to each side of an inequality, so if $a \leqslant b$, then $a + c \leqslant b + c$ and $a - c \leqslant b - c$.
- You can multiply or divide each side of an inequality by a positive number, so if $a \leqslant b$ and $c > 0$, then $ac \leqslant bc$.
- But when you multiply or divide by a negative number the inequality sign reverses, so if $a \leqslant b$ and $c < 0$, then $ac \geqslant bc$.
- You can represent the solution of a linear inequality on a number line.

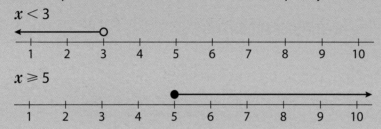

$x < 3$

$x \geqslant 5$

(1) Solve the inequalities.
Represent the solution set using a number line.

a $x + 2 < 9$

b $x - 5 \geqslant 13$

c $3x + 2 > 14$

d $3x - 8 \geqslant x + 4$

e $-3x \leqslant -12$

f $5 - x > 2$

(2) Find the values of x that satisfy both inequalities.
Represent the solution set using a number line.

a $3x + 4 \geqslant 2x + 3$
$6(x - 1) \leqslant 2(x + 5)$

b $2x - 18 < 21 - x$
$2x + 5 \geqslant 15 - 3x$

c $-2x - 5 > x + 19$
$2x - 27 > 3 - x$

d $4x + 3 < 6x + 2$
$8x - 2 < 7 - 4x$

e $12 - x \leqslant 6 + x$
$5(2x - 3) \leqslant 6x + 1$

f $3x + 2 \leqslant 17 - 7x$
$2x - 9 \leqslant 17 + 15x$

TASK 5: Linear inequalities in two variables

 Points to remember

⊙ The region representing an inequality can be shown on a coordinate grid.

⊙ To show the region, first draw the graph, using a solid or dotted line as appropriate.

⊙ Solid lines are used for $\geqslant$ and $\leqslant$ and dotted lines for $<$ and $>$.

⊙ Check points on each side of the line to see which region represents the inequality and then shade the unwanted region.

You need a copy of **A7.1 Resource sheet A5.1**.

1 Write the inequalities representing the **unshaded** region of the graphs.

a 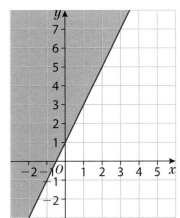   **b**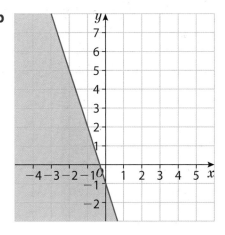

2 Use **A7.1 Resource sheet A5.1**.

For each set of inequalities, use a new pair of axes from −5 to 5.

Represent all the points satisfying each set of inequalities by shading the unwanted region on a graph.

a $y \leqslant 2$ and $x \geqslant 5$

b $y \geqslant -1$ and $x < 3$

c $-1 < x \leqslant 4$ and $-2 \leqslant y < 0$

d $-3 \leqslant x \leqslant 2$ and $-4 \leqslant y < 1.5$

e $y \geqslant -x$ and $y \leqslant x + 3$ and $y \geqslant 3x - 4$

f $y \geqslant -3$ and $y < 2x + 2$ and $y < -2x + 2$

TASK 6: Optimisation problems

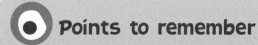

⊙ Points to remember

⊙ Many real-life problems can be modelled using inequalities:
  - First decide what the variables are and assign letters to them.
  - Read through the problem and form a set of inequalities.
  - Draw the relevant graphs and shade any unwanted regions.
  - Find all the possible solutions in the unshaded region, then decide which of the possible solutions gives the best solution.

1. Oliver and his wife Mary make pottery.
   Oliver can make 10 vases and 4 water jugs in an hour.
   He is paid £20 an hour.
   Mary can make 6 vases and 4 water jugs in an hour.
   She is paid £15 an hour.
   Oliver and Mary need to make at least 60 vases and 32 water jugs.
   Let x be the number of hours worked by Oliver.
   Let y be the number of hours worked by Mary.

   a Write two inequalities in x and y.

   b Draw graphs and shade the unwanted regions.

   c What is the least number of hours that Oliver and Mary should work to minimise the costs?

2. The Wave-Rider Surfboard Company makes two types of surfboard.
   Type A requires 4 hours of machine time and 6 hours of shapers' time.
   Type B requires 3 hours of machine time and 8 hours of shapers' time.
   Each day there are 24 hours of machine time available and 50 hours of shapers' time.
   The profit on a Type A board is £25 and on a Type B board is £32.
   Let x be the number of Type A surfboards made in a day and y the number of Type B.

   a Write two inequalities in x and y.

   b Draw graphs and shade the unwanted regions.

   c How many of each type of surfboard should be made in a day to maximise the profits?

Decimals and accuracy

TASK 1: Significant figures

⊙ Points to remember

- The **first significant figure** is the first non-zero digit.
- A number **rounded to one significant figure** has only one non-zero digit.
- In general, estimates of calculations are made by rounding numbers to one significant figure but sometimes other approximations of the numbers in a calculation are more sensible.
- In **exact calculations**, only the final answer is rounded, not the intermediate steps.
- In **approximate calculations**, the numbers can be rounded at any stage.
- Choose appropriate degrees of accuracy for answers to problems, based on the context. The most significant 2 or 3 digits are usually enough.

Example

Estimate the value of $(5.6 \times 279.8) \div 0.42$.

Round each number to 1 significant figure.

$$(5.6 \times 279.8) \div 0.42 \approx (6 \times 300) \div 0.4$$
$$= 1800 \div 0.4$$
$$= 4500$$

1 Copy and complete this table.

Number	Rounded to 1 s.f.	Rounded to 2 s.f.	Rounded to 3 s.f.
48.76			
0.7683			
11.32			
1449.9			
0.018 75			

Estimate then calculate the value of each expression.

    i Work out an approximate value for each expression.

    ii Calculate the answer. Write all the figures on your calculator display.

    iii Write the answer correct to a sensible degree of accuracy.

a $\dfrac{4.5^3}{6.67 \times 9.44}$ **b** $\dfrac{3.46 \times 5.98}{5.50^2}$ **c** $\dfrac{9.1^2 + \sqrt{398}}{62}$ **d** $\dfrac{\sqrt[3]{345} \times 4.8^2}{45 + \sqrt{4.1}}$

3 Here is some information.

Number of trees needed to make 1 tonne of paper	15
Number of households in the UK	24 million
Typical mass of a piece of junk mail	50 g
Number of secondary schools in the UK	4000
Typical mass of an exercise book	100 g

Estimate how many trees are cut down each year for the production of:

a exercise books for UK secondary schools;

b the junk mail sent to UK households.

Write down any extra assumptions that you make and the calculations that you do.

TASK 2: Standard form

 Did you know that…?

Here are some examples of **big numbers**:

- The number of neuron connections in the human brain is estimated at 10^{14}.

- The number of cells in the human body is more than 10^{14}.

- The number of bits of data on a hard disk is huge. 125 gigabytes is about 10^{11} bytes.

- The number of atoms in one mole of substance is approximately 6.022×10^{23}. This is known as **Avogadro's constant**.

Avogadro (1776–1856) was an Italian count who worked on physics and mathematics.

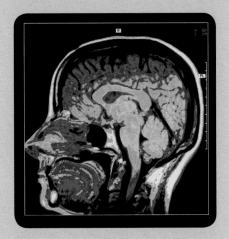

Points to remember

⊙ A number in **standard form** is of the form $A \times 10^n$, where $1 \leqslant A < 10$ and n is an integer.

⊙ The key for entering numbers in standard form is usually $\boxed{\text{EXP}}$ or $\boxed{\wedge}$. Use the negative key $\boxed{-}$ or the sign change key $\boxed{+/-}$ for negative powers.

Examples

To enter 3.75×10^4, press:

$\boxed{3}\boxed{.}\boxed{7}\boxed{5}\boxed{\text{EXP}}\boxed{4}$

or:

$\boxed{3}\boxed{.}\boxed{7}\boxed{5}\boxed{\times}\boxed{1}\boxed{0}\boxed{\wedge}\boxed{4}$

To enter 2.8×10^{-3}, press:

$\boxed{2}\boxed{.}\boxed{8}\boxed{\text{EXP}}\boxed{+/-}\boxed{3}$

or:

$\boxed{2}\boxed{.}\boxed{8}\boxed{\times}\boxed{1}\boxed{0}\boxed{\wedge}\boxed{+/-}\boxed{3}$

(1) Write in standard form:

   a 38 000 000   **b** 27 400

   c 0.000 000 92   **d** 0.0005

(2) Write as ordinary numbers:

   a 7×10^9 **b** 3.65×10^{-4}

   c 6.79×10^{-2} **d** 8.04×10^{-1}

(3) Write in standard form:

   a 29×10^3 **b** 35.8×10^{-5}

   c 0.25×10^{-3} **d** 176×10^{-4}

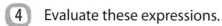

(4) Evaluate these expressions.
    Give your answers in standard form correct to 3 significant figures.

   a $(2.8 \times 10^4) \times (4.7 \times 10^8)$ **b** $(5.86 \times 10^{21}) \times (7.88 \times 10^{-12})$

   c $(8.35 \times 10^{-4}) \div (1.5 \times 10^7)$ **d** $(4.25 \times 10^{-11}) \div (9.7 \times 10^{-3})$

(5) An atomic particle travels at a speed of 4.2×10^6 metres per second.
    It has a lifetime of 3.86×10^5 seconds.
    How far does it travel in its lifetime?

(6) The mass of an atom of uranium is 3.98×10^{-22} grams.
    How many atoms are there in 4.5 kilograms of uranium?

TASK 3: Accuracy of measurements

 Did you know that...?

Metric units are used in nearly every country of the world. The USA is one of only three countries where **imperial units** are still used.

In 1999 NASA lost a $125 million Mars orbiter because one engineering team used SI metric units while another used imperial units for a calculation.

Points to remember

⊙ Measurements may be inaccurate by **up to half a unit** in either direction, e.g. '4 kg to the nearest kilogram' has a least possible mass of 3.5 kg and a greatest possible mass of 4.5 kg.

⊙ The **upper and lower bounds** are the upper and lower limits of accuracy.

① Write the maximum and minimum possible values for each of these.

   a The height of a door is 2.10 m to the nearest centimetre.

   b 25 000 people watched the match to the nearest 1000.

   c There is 80 g of flour in a recipe to the nearest 10 grams.

   d An aeroplane flies at 380 mph to the nearest 10 mph.

   e A jug holds 0.5 litres of water to the nearest millilitre.

   f The area of the lawn is 60 m² to the nearest square metre.

   g The sugar weighs 400 g to 1 significant figure.

   h The sugar weighs 400 g to 2 significant figures.

   i The sugar weighs 400 g to 3 significant figures.

② For each rounded number, write the lower and upper bounds.

   a 15.0 (to 1 decimal place)   **b** 0.08 (to 2 decimal places)

   c 1200 (to 3 significant figures)   **d** 0.0400 (to 3 significant figures)

   e 100 (to the nearest whole number)   **f** 500 000 (to the nearest 10 000)

③ Ali wants to lay a path of paving slabs.
The path is to be 30 m long to the nearest 10 cm.

   Ali buys 76 slabs that are 40 cm long to the nearest cm.
Explain why he should have bought one more slab to be certain of having enough.

TASK 4: Upper and lower bounds

 Did you know that...?

In 1791 the length of 1 metre was officially defined by the French Academy of Sciences as one ten millionth of the line of longitude that runs from the equator to the North Pole through Paris.

The definition was changed in 1960 to the wavelength of light emitted by the krypton-86 atom. It was redefined again in 1983 as the distance that light travels in a vacuum in $\frac{1}{299\,792\,458}$ seconds.

This remains the definition today.

 Points to remember

⊙ For two numbers a and b with bounds $a_{min} \leqslant a < a_{max}$ and $b_{min} \leqslant b < b_{max}$:

Operation	Maximum	Minimum
$a + b$	$a_{max} + b_{max}$	$a_{min} + b_{min}$
$a - b$	$a_{max} - b_{min}$	$a_{min} - b_{max}$
$a \times b$	$a_{max} \times b_{max}$	$a_{min} \times b_{min}$
$a \div b$	$a_{max} \div b_{min}$	$a_{min} \div b_{max}$

1. The world's longest skateboard is a cuboid that measures 11.14 m long, 2.63 m wide and 1.10 m thick, all to the nearest centimetre. It was completed in 2005 in Massachusetts, USA. Find the greatest and least possible values for the volume of the skateboard.

2. A rectangle has an area of 180 cm², to the nearest 10 cm². The length is 15 cm, to the nearest cm.

   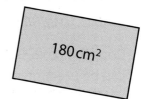

   a What is the greatest possible width of the rectangle?

   b What is the least possible width of the rectangle?

3. A mug holds 200 ml water to the nearest 10 ml.
   A jug holds 1900 ml to the nearest 100 ml.
   Daisy says that she can only fill nine mugs of water from the jug.
   She could be wrong. Explain why.

4. $x = 10$, $y = 20$ and $z = 30$. All values are to the nearest whole number.
   Work out the upper and lower bounds of:

   a xy b $z \div x$ c $xz - y$ d $z^2 - x^2$

TASK 5: Dimensions

 Points to remember

⊙ Numbers like 4 or π have no **dimensions**.

⊙ The circumference of a circle with diameter d is πd.
The expression πd is a number × a length. It has the dimension *length*.

⊙ The area of a rectangle of length l and width w is lw.
The expression lw has the dimension *length × length*.

⊙ The volume of a cuboid of length l, width w and height h is lwh.
The expression lwh has the dimension *length × length × length*.

1 The expressions below can be used to calculate lengths, areas or volumes of some shapes.
The letters a, b and c are lengths.
Three of the expressions can be used to calculate an area.
Which three are they?

A $\pi(a + b)$ **B** $\dfrac{a^2c}{2}$ **C** $c(a + b)$ **D** πab

E $bc(a + b)$ **F** $4a$ **G** $\dfrac{ab}{c}$ **H** $\dfrac{bc}{2}$

2 p, q and r are lengths.

Expression	Length	Area	Volume	None of these
$\pi p^2 q$				
$\pi q^2 + 2r$				
$2pr$				

Copy the table. Put a tick (✓) in the correct column to show whether the expression can be used for length, area, volume or none of these.

3 Here are six expressions.

A $x + y + z$ **B** $2x + 2z$ **C** $4x^2z$

D $3xy$ **E** $2x^2 + yz$ **F** $xy(y + 2z)$

x, y and z are lengths.

a Two of the expressions represent areas. Which two are they?

b Two of the expressions represent volumes. Which two are they?

Enquiry 1

TASK 1: Sampling

 Points to remember

⊙ **Sampling** is a way of finding out about the population as a whole without asking each person.

⊙ You need to decide which sampling method to use:
  – in a **random sample**, each member of the population has an equal chance of being chosen;
  – in a **systematic or selective sample**, every nth member is chosen from a random starting point;
  – in a **stratified sample**, the population is divided into groups, then each group is randomly or selectively sampled.

(1) Ellen's school has 900 pupils.
She wants to sample 45 of them for a project.
Describe in detail a way of choosing a sample of this size from the school population using each of the three different sampling methods.

(2) A manufacturer of garden gnomes produces these model numbers in one day.

Model number	001	004	006	007	010
Number	600	300	500	400	200

He needs to test 100 of his gnomes for paint chips before they leave his factory.
Describe how he should choose a sample.

(3) Use a calculator to generate sets of random numbers between 1 and 100 with 5, 10, 15 and 20 numbers in them.

  a Write down the smallest number in each set.

  b Write down the largest number in each set.

  c How do you expect your results to differ when you compare with sets generated by others in your class?

TASK 2: Planning and collecting data

① Measure the reaction times of ten different people and write them in your book.

You could do this using a computer. There are reaction times online, for example, at **www.mathsisfun.com/games/games–2.html**

Alternatively, make a reaction timer using a piece of card, approximately 20 cm by 5 cm.

Mark off the distances on the card as shown.
Write the corresponding number of milliseconds by each mark.
For example 12.3 cm from the bottom is 180 milliseconds.

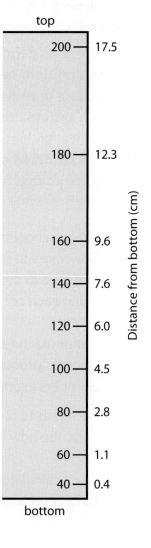

top	
200 —	17.5
180 —	12.3
160 —	9.6
140 —	7.6
120 —	6.0
100 —	4.5
80 —	2.8
60 —	1.1
40 —	0.4
bottom	

Distance from bottom (cm)

Instructions for use

▶ Hold your reaction timer at the top.

▶ Ask someone to hold their fingers level with the bottom edge of the timer, but not touching it.

▶ Drop the reaction timer without warning.
Ask the person to try and catch it between a finger and their thumb.

▶ Read off their time from the card.

TASK 3: Drawing histograms

 Points to remember

- A **frequency diagram** represents grouped discrete data. The class intervals, and the bars, are of equal width and there are gaps between the bars. Each bar has a label below it.
- A **histogram** represents grouped continuous data. There is a scale on the horizontal axis rather than a label under each bar. There are no gaps between the bars. When the class intervals are of equal width, the bars are of equal width.
- Frequency diagrams and histograms can be used to:
    - look at the shapes of distributions;
    - look for patterns;
    - compare sets of data.

Example

The **frequency table** shows some data on the reaction times of Australian Year 5 pupils.

Time (seconds)	Frequency
$0.2 \leqslant t < 0.3$	9
$0.3 \leqslant t < 0.4$	37
$0.4 \leqslant t < 0.5$	33
$0.5 \leqslant t < 0.6$	5
$0.6 \leqslant t < 0.7$	2
$0.7 \leqslant t < 0.8$	1

The data is also shown as a **histogram**.

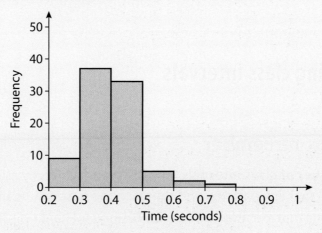

Data source: www.abs.gov.au/websitedbs/cashome.nsf/home/home

You will need a pencil, ruler and graph paper.

① The tables contain data on the reaction time for Year 5 and Year 10 pupils in New Zealand (data source: **www.censusatschool.org**).
100 pupils from each of Years 5 and 10 were selected randomly.

Year 5		Year 10	
Time (s)	Frequency	Time (s)	Frequency
$0.2 \leqslant x < 0.3$	0	$0.2 \leqslant x < 0.3$	4
$0.3 \leqslant x < 0.4$	5	$0.3 \leqslant x < 0.4$	30
$0.4 \leqslant x < 0.5$	28	$0.4 \leqslant x < 0.5$	33
$0.5 \leqslant x < 0.6$	10	$0.5 \leqslant x < 0.6$	13
$0.6 \leqslant x < 0.7$	13	$0.6 \leqslant x < 0.7$	6
$0.7 \leqslant x < 0.8$	5	$0.7 \leqslant x < 0.8$	3
$0.8 \leqslant x < 0.9$	2	$0.8 \leqslant x < 0.9$	2
$0.9 \leqslant x < 1.0$	4	$0.9 \leqslant x < 1.0$	4

a The data was cleaned.
What sort of errors do you think the data contained?

b Why do you think more of the Year 5 pupils' data was removed in the cleaning process?
Explain your answer.

c What question could you answer using this data?

d Draw a histogram for each of the sets of data.

e Write down what the histograms show and the answer to your question in part **c**.

TASK 4: Choosing class intervals

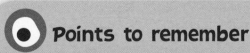

Points to remember

⊙ Choose the **number of class intervals** for a histogram carefully:
– too few means that any patterns and trends in the data will be hidden;
– too many means that the graph will be confusing and hard to interpret.

You will need a pencil, ruler and graph paper.

 1 In the example for Task 3 some data on reaction times of a sample of Australian pupils is displayed as a grouped frequency table and as a histogram.

Here is the raw data for that histogram:

0.25	0.27	0.28	0.28	0.28	0.28	0.29	0.29	0.29	0.30
0.31	0.31	0.31	0.31	0.32	0.32	0.32	0.32	0.32	0.32
0.32	0.32	0.33	0.33	0.33	0.34	0.34	0.35	0.35	0.35
0.35	0.36	0.36	0.36	0.36	0.36	0.37	0.37	0.37	0.37
0.37	0.38	0.39	0.39	0.39	0.39	0.40	0.40	0.40	0.40
0.40	0.40	0.40	0.40	0.42	0.42	0.42	0.42	0.42	0.43
0.43	0.43	0.43	0.43	0.44	0.44	0.44	0.45	0.45	0.45
0.45	0.46	0.46	0.46	0.47	0.47	0.48	0.48	0.49	0.51
0.53	0.54	0.55	0.55	0.6	0.68	0.75			

a Draw a grouped frequency table for the data using the class intervals:
$0.25 \leqslant t < 0.30, 0.30 \leqslant t < 0.35$, etc.
What is the class width?

b Draw a histogram to represent this data using the class intervals in part **a**.

c Draw another grouped frequency table, this time with the class intervals:
$0.20 \leqslant t < 0.40, 0.40 \leqslant t < 0.60$, etc.
What is the class width?

d Draw a histogram to represent this data using the class intervals in part **c**.

e Which is the better choice of class interval? Why?

TASK 5: Using histograms

● Points to remember

⊙ When the class intervals are unequal, the histogram is drawn so that the area of each rectangle or bar is proportional to the frequency.

⊙ The height of each rectangle is the **frequency density** of the class and the vertical axis is labelled 'frequency density'.

⊙ Frequency density $= \dfrac{\text{frequency}}{\text{class width}}$.

Example

This histogram shows the finish times in the Bolsover Mizuno 10 km race in 2007. The data comes from the race results on **www.thepowerof10.info**.

Look carefully at the histogram. The class intervals vary.

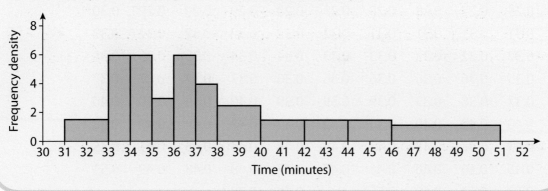

You will need a pencil, ruler and graph paper.

1 The tables below show the data in the histogram grouped in two other races.
Again, the class intervals are not equal.
Draw histograms with frequency density on the vertical axis for each of the races.

a

Time (minutes)	Frequency	Frequency density
$31 \leqslant x < 32$	3	3
$32 \leqslant x < 33$	4	4
$33 \leqslant x < 34$	4	4
$34 \leqslant x < 35$	10	10
$35 \leqslant x < 36$	2	2
$36 \leqslant x < 37$	2	2
$37 \leqslant x < 38$	2	2
$38 \leqslant x < 40$	8	4
$40 \leqslant x < 42$	4	2
$42 \leqslant x < 56$	4	0.29

b

Time (minutes)	Frequency	Frequency density
$35 \leqslant x < 36$	2	2
$36 \leqslant x < 37$	2	2
$37 \leqslant x < 38$	2	2
$38 \leqslant x < 39$	4	4
$39 \leqslant x < 40$	3	3
$40 \leqslant x < 41$	3	3
$41 \leqslant x < 42$	2	2
$42 \leqslant x < 44$	4	2
$44 \leqslant x < 46$	4	2
$46 \leqslant x < 50$	4	1
$50 < x < 58$	2	0.25

2 Write two sentences comparing the finish times for the two races.

TASK 6: Moving averages

 Points to remember

⊙ A **time series graph** shows a set of data collected over a period of time.

⊙ To look for trends in the data, plot the **moving averages**.

⊙ The set of **5-point moving averages** is the mean of the 1st to 5th values, followed by the mean of the 2nd to 6th values, followed by the mean of the 3rd to 7th values, and so on.

Example

The **table** and **time series graph** show the cups of soup sold by a cafe over 3 years.

Season	Year 1	Year 2	Year 3
Winter (W)	5900	5500	5100
Spring (Sp)	2400	2000	1600
Summer (Su)	1600	1200	1200
Autumn (A)	5700	5300	4900

Has the number of cups of soup sold increased or decreased over the three years?

To find out, calculate the **moving average**.

The mean of the first four values
(W, Sp, Su, A of Year 1)

$$= \frac{5900 + 2400 + 1600 + 5700}{4} = 3900 \text{ cups.}$$

The mean of the next four values (Sp, Su, A of Year 1 and W of Year 2) = 3800 cups.

The mean of the next four values (Su, A of Year 1 and W, Sp of Year 2) = 3700 cups, etc.

Since four consecutive values are used each time, they are called **4-point moving averages**.

Plot the moving averages on the graph, and join the points.

Each moving average is plotted at the midpoint of the time period it covers. So the 1st moving average of 3900 cups is plotted halfway between Spring and Summer of Year 1.

It is clear from this that the number of cups of soup sold decreased slowly over the three-year period.

This is called the **trend** of the graph.

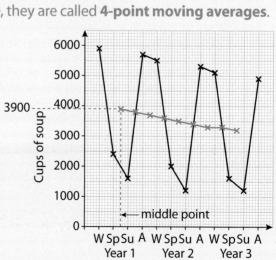

You will need a pencil, ruler and graph paper.

1 The table shows the sales of ice cream from a kiosk during each day of one week.

	Mon	Tues	Wed	Thurs	Fri	Sat	Sun
Number of people	170	380	530	560	500	1250	1160

  a Calculate the set of 3-point moving averages for this data.

  b Comment on the trend of the sales of ice cream throughout the week.

2 Peter buys logs for his wood burning stove.

The table shows what he spent in £ on logs over a three-year period.

Season	Year 1	Year 2	Year 3
Winter (W)	218	228	242
Spring (Sp)	163	166	138
Summer (Su)	68	43	38
Autumn (A)	179	139	122

  a Plot this information on a time series graph.

  b Work out the 4-point moving averages for the three years.

  c On your time series graph plot the moving averages.

  d Comment on the trend in Peter's expenditure on logs during this period.

Measures and mensuration

TASK 1: Arcs and sectors of circles

 Did you know that...?

It is only during the last 2500 years that people have thought that the Earth is a sphere. Before that, they thought it was a disc with the Mediterranean Sea flowing across it.

It is not known who first suggested that Earth is a sphere but about 500 BC **Pythagoras** taught his followers that it was so.

The Greek, **Eratosthenes**, was the first to measure the circumference of the Earth about 200 BC. He noticed that on the longest day of the year the Sun shone directly down a well in the Egyptian city of Syene.

He also knew that in his home town of Alexandria the Sun cast a shadow beside an upright pillar and that this meant that the angle of elevation of the Sun was $\frac{1}{50}$ of a full circle.

Statue of Pythagoras, Samos, Greece

Eratosthenes concluded that the distance from Alexandria to Syene must be $\frac{1}{50}$ of the total circumference of the Earth. He estimated the distance between the cities as 5000 stadia (roughly 500 miles or 800 km). This implied a circumference of the Earth of about 40 000 km, which was remarkably accurate.

Here are some facts about the Earth. The numbers are rounded.

Diameter at the equator	12 760 km
Diameter at the poles	12 710 km
Circumference at the equator	40 077 km
Total surface area	504 190 000 km^2
Land area	147 220 000 km^2
Sea area	356 970 000 km^2
Mass	5.98 × 10^{24} kg

The Moon began orbiting Earth about 4.53 billion years ago.

Points to remember

- **Circumference of circle** $= \pi \times$ diameter $= 2 \times \pi \times$ radius
- **Arc length** $=$ (angle $\div$ 360) $\times$ circumference of the circle
- **Area of circle** $= \pi \times$ radius $\times$ radius $= \pi r^2$
- **Area of sector** $=$ (angle $\div$ 360) $\times$ area of circle

Take $\pi = 3.142$ or use the π key on your calculator.
Where appropriate, give your answers correct to three significant figures.

1. For each circle, calculate **i** the length of the arc and **ii** the area of the sector.

   a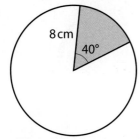

   b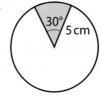

   c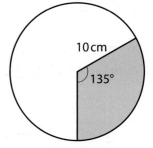

2. Calculate **i** the total perimeter and **ii** the area of these sectors.

   a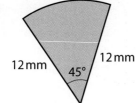

   b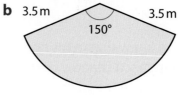

3. A quadrant, of radius 6 cm, has the same area as a complete circle of radius r cm.

   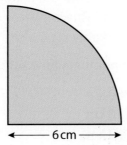

   What is the radius of the complete circle? Show your working.

TASK 2: Circle problems

Points to remember

- **Area of segment** = area of sector − area of isosceles triangle
- To convert to a smaller unit, e.g. cm^2 to mm^2, **multiply** by the conversion factor.
- To convert to a larger unit, e.g. mm^2 to cm^2, **divide** by the conversion factor.
- When problems involve areas of parts of circles, look for the semicircles, quadrants, sectors and segments that could help you.
- You may need to use Pythagoras' theorem or trigonometry.

Take $\pi = 3.142$ or use the π key on your calculator.
Where appropriate, give your answers correct to three significant figures.

1. Find the area of each shaded segment.

   a
   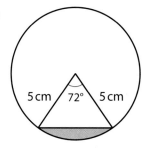

   b
   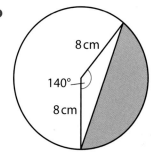

2. The scales of a large pink fish are made up of the arcs of semicircles with radius 2 cm.

   What is the area of one of the scales?

3. The diagram shows three circles touching each other. The diameters of the three circles all lie on the same straight line.
   The area shaded green in the large circle is equal to the area in blue of the middle-sized circle.
   Find the ratio of the diameters of the three circles.

   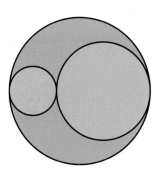

TASK 3: Volume of 3D shapes

Points to remember

- **Volume of a prism**
  area of cross-section × length, or area of base × height
- **Volume of a cylinder**, radius r, height h
  area of cross-section × length, or area of base × height, or $V = \pi r^2 h$
- **Volume of pyramid** is $\frac{1}{3}$ × area of base × height
- **Volume of cone**, base radius r, height h,
  $\frac{1}{3}$ × area of base × height, or $V = \frac{1}{3}\pi r^2 h$
- **Volume of a sphere**, radius r, is $V = \frac{4}{3}\pi r^3$

Take $\pi = 3.142$ or use the π key on your calculator.

1. The diagram shows a metal pipe of length 1 m.
   It has an internal diameter of 2.8 cm, and an external diameter of 3.2 cm.
   Calculate the volume of metal in the pipe to the nearest cubic centimetre.

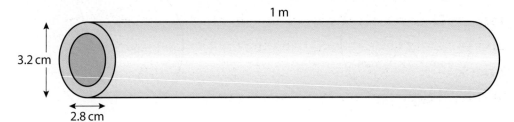

2. The areas of the faces of a cuboid box
   are 4, 16 and 25 square centimetres.

   What is the volume of the box?

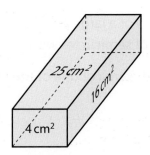

3. The radius of a sphere is equal to the radius of the base of a cone.
   The sphere and the cone have equal volumes.
   Find the relationship between the cone's height h and its base radius r.

4. A cylindrical vase holds 2 litres of water when it is full.
   The height of the vase is 25 cm. Calculate the radius of its base.
   Give your answer correct to one decimal place.

TASK 4: Surface area of 3D shapes

 Did you know that...?

The surface area of a sphere can be used to work out a formula for its volume.

Imagine the sphere is filled with small pyramids, each with height r and with its apex at the centre of the sphere. If the pyramid is small enough, its base is almost flat and its volume is $\frac{1}{3}$ base area $\times r$.

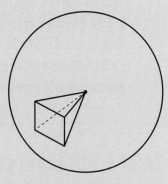

The volume of the sphere is the sum of the volumes of all these small pyramids, or $\frac{1}{3}$ total base area $\times r$.

The total base area of all the pyramids is the surface area of the sphere, which is $4\pi r^2$. So the volume V of the sphere is $V = \frac{1}{3} \times 4\pi r^2 \times r$, which simplifies to $\frac{4}{3}\pi r^3$.

 Points to remember

⊙ The surface area of many 3D shapes can be worked out from their nets.

⊙ **Total surface area of cylinder**, radius r, height h, is $A = 2\pi rh + 2\pi r^2$.

⊙ **Curved surface area of cone**, base radius r, slant height l, is πrl.

⊙ **Total surface area of cone**, base radius r, slant height l, is $A = \pi r^2 + \pi rl$.

⊙ **Surface area of a sphere**, radius r, is $A = 4\pi r^2$.

Take $\pi = 3.142$ or use the π key on your calculator.

1. The radius of the base of a cone is 4.3 cm and its slant height is 9.7 cm.
   Calculate its total surface area. Give your answers correct to three significant figures.

2. Find the cost of the material for making a spherical air balloon, 32 m in circumference, at £16 per square metre.

3. The turret of a castle is in the shape of a cone 6 m high and 9 m in diameter.

   The roof tiles of the turret are to be replaced at a cost of £35 per square metre plus VAT at 17.5%.

   Work out the cost of replacing the tiles.

(4) An oil storage tank is in the shape of a cylinder. Its outside surface (walls and top) are to be painted.

The diameter of the tank is 12.8 metres.
The height of the tank is 7.2 metres.
1 litre of paint covers 2.5 m² of surface.
The cost of paint is £2.95 per litre.
Calculate the cost of paint needed to paint the outside of the tank.

TASK 5: Problem solving

 Points to remember

Some problem solving strategies to try are:

⊙ draw a diagram or make a model;

⊙ use the properties of shapes and mark equal lengths and equal angles;

⊙ identify the variables and write a formula;

⊙ use proportional reasoning;

⊙ predict and test;

⊙ try a simpler problem;

⊙ think backwards.

(1) A railway tunnel is semicircular.
It has a diameter of 10 metres.
The track is 2 metres from one side of the tunnel.

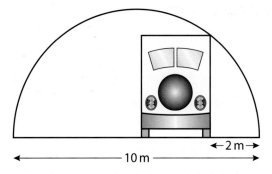

What is the maximum height of a train?

2 *2002 level 8*

This prism was made from three cuboids.

a Show that the area of the cross-section of the prism is $24x^2 + 3xy$.

b The volume of the prism is $3x^2(8x + y)$.

What is the depth?

Show your working.

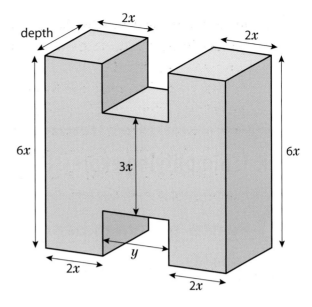

Not drawn accurately

3 *2000 Exceptional performance*

A manufacturer makes party hats shaped like hollow cones.

To make the hats she cuts pieces of card which are sectors of a circle, radius 24 cm.

The angle of the sector is 135°.

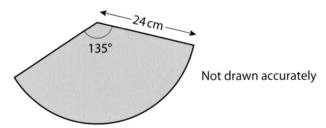

Not drawn accurately

a Show that the arc length of the sector is 18π cm.

b The edges of the sector meet exactly with no overlap. Calculate the vertical height of the completed hat.

Show your working.

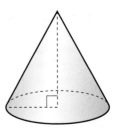

Expressions and formulae

TASK 1: Simplifying expressions

Points to remember

- Try to **simplify** algebraic expressions:
  - multiply out any brackets and collect like terms;
  - divide the numerator and denominator of any fractions by any common factors.
- To multiply two powers of x, add the indices, so $x^a \times x^b = x^{a+b}$.
- To divide two powers of x, subtract the indices, so $x^a \div x^b = x^{a-b}$.
- To raise a power of x to a power, multiply the indices, so $(x^a)^b = x^{a \times b}$.

(1) Simplify these expressions.

   a $y^9 \div y^{-11}$ **b** $r^{-8} \times r^{-3}$ **c** $a^{-3} \div a^{-10}$

   d $a^{\frac{1}{5}} \times a^{\frac{4}{5}}$ **e** $b^{\frac{7}{2}} \times b^{\frac{5}{2}}$ **f** $a^2 b^{\frac{1}{2}} \div a^4 b^{\frac{3}{2}}$

(2) Expand the brackets and, where possible, simplify the answers.

   a $bc(a + b^2 c)$ **b** $x(y^2 - 2z^2) - xy^2$

   c $e(f + g) - e(f - g)$ **d** $p(q^2 + r^2) - r(pr + q^2)$

   e $3r(s + t) - 2s(r + 2s)$ **f** $3x(4x^2 + 2y) - 2y(3x - y^2)$

(3) Simplify these expressions

   a $ax^3 \times a^3 x^6$ **b** $q^3 p^4 \times p^{-2}$ **c** $a^{-2} b^3 \times a^3 b^{-5}$

   d $x^2 y^4 \times x^3 q$ **e** $3a^{-3} \times 6a^2$ **f** $9x^3 y^3 \times 3xy$

(4) Simplify these expressions.

   a $\dfrac{z^3}{z}$ **b** $\dfrac{a^5 b}{a^2}$ **c** $\dfrac{2r^4}{6r^6}$

   d $\dfrac{m^{-5}}{m^{-4}}$ **e** $\dfrac{2m^3 n^2}{4mn}$ **f** $\dfrac{x^6 y^2}{x^4 y^4}$

TASK 2: Expanding brackets

 Points to remember

- A number or letter outside a bracket has to be multiplied by everything inside the bracket, e.g.

  $4(a + 7) = 4a + 28$ and $a(a + 5) = a^2 + 5a$.

- To **expand the product of two linear expressions**, multiply everything in one bracket by everything in the other bracket.

- You can use a multiplication grid to help you to multiply out brackets.

- Alternatively, use **FOIL** to multiply **F**irst terms, **O**utside terms, **I**nside terms, **L**ast terms, e.g.

  $(a + 3)(a + 5) = a^2 + 3a + 5a + 15 = a^2 + 8a + 15$

  $(a + 3)(a - 5) = a^2 + 3a - 5a - 15 = a^2 - 2a - 15$

  $(a - 3)(a + 5) = a^2 - 3a + 5a - 15 = a^2 + 2a - 15$

  $(a - 3)(a - 5) = a^2 - 3a - 5a + 15 = a^2 - 8a + 15$

1   Expand the brackets in these expressions.

     a $(a + 5)(a + 7)$ **b** $(b + 6)(b + 8)$

     c $(3x + 1)(2x + 4)$ **d** $(6y + 9)(2y + 1)$

2   Match the expanded brackets on cards A to D to the expressions on cards W to Z.

A $(a - 5)(a - 7)$	**W** $12a^2 - 17a + 6$
B $(3a - 2)(4a - 3)$	**X** $12a^2 - 34a + 20$
C $(a - 6)(a - 8)$	**Y** $a^2 - 12a + 35$
D $(2a - 4)(6a - 5)$	**Z** $a^2 - 14a + 48$

3   Expand the brackets in these expressions.

     a $(a + 5)(a - 7)$ **b** $(b - 6)(b + 8)$

     c $(2x - 1)(5x + 2)$ **d** $(7y + 2)(3y - 4)$

TASK 3: Factorising expressions

Points to remember

- A **quadratic expression** can sometimes be written as the product of two linear expressions, e.g. $a^2 - 8a + 15 = (a - 3)(a - 5)$
- To **factorise** the quadratic expression $x^2 + bx + c$, find a factor pair of c with a sum of b:
  - if c is positive, both signs in the brackets are the same as the sign of b, i.e.
    for c positive and b positive, the brackets are $(x + \ )(x + \ )$
    for c positive and b negative, the brackets are $(x - \ )(x - \ )$
  - if c is negative, the brackets are $(x + \ )(x - \ )$.

1. Factorise these expressions.

   a $x^2 + 4x + 3$ **b** $x^2 + 10x + 16$ **c** $x^2 + 9x + 20$ **d** $x^2 + 9x + 14$

2. Write whether each factorisation is right or wrong.
   If the factorisation is wrong, write the correct factorisation.

   a $x^2 - 5x + 4 = (x - 2)(x - 2)$ **b** $x^2 - 7x + 10 = (x + 5)(x + 2)$

   c $x^2 - 13x + 42 = (x - 7)(x - 6)$ **d** $x^2 - 10x + 9 = (x + 9)(x - 1)$

3. Factorise these expressions.

   a $x^2 + 6x - 7$ **b** $x^2 - 7x - 18$ **c** $x^2 - 4x - 21$ **d** $x^2 - 6x - 16$

TASK 4: Working with formulae

Points to remember

- A **formula** is a way of expressing a relationship using symbols.
- When a formula is written as $d = st$, then d is called the **subject** of the formula.
- You can rearrange a formula to make a different letter the subject, e.g. $s = \dfrac{d}{t}$ or $t = \dfrac{d}{s}$
- When you substitute values into a formula, check that any quantities are in the correct units.

1 **a** The length l of an arc of a circle of radius r and angle x at the centre is

$l = \dfrac{x}{360} \times 2\pi r.$

Find l when $r = 5\,\text{cm}$ and $x = 60°$. Use a value of 3.14 for π.

b A pyramid has a square base with side a and perpendicular height h.

Its volume V is $V = \frac{1}{3}a^2h$.

Find a when $V = 24\,\text{cm}^3$ and $h = 8\,\text{cm}$

c A car starts with velocity u and travels a distance s with constant acceleration a. Its final velocity v is given by $v^2 = u^2 + 2as$.

Find v when $u = 3\,\text{ms}^{-1}$, $a = 2\,\text{ms}^{-2}$ and $s = 10\,\text{m}$.

2 Make the letter in brackets the subject of each formula.

a $C = 2\pi r$ (r) **b** $V = wlh$ (h) **c** $\tan x = \dfrac{O}{A}$ (O) **d** $\tan x = \dfrac{O}{A}$ (A)

TASK 5: Investigations

 Points to remember

⊙ One approach to an **investigation** is to try lots of examples, look for patterns, make a conjecture, test it, then try to justify the result.

⊙ Another approach is to identify and define the variables and set up and manipulate an expression or equation to prove a result.

⊙ A good solution to an investigation is concise and elegant as well as clear and well explained.

① Investigate how the sequences below relate to the sequence of triangular numbers. Use this relationship to find the nth term of each sequence.

   a 2, 6, 12, 20, 30, …   **b** 2, 4, 7, 11, 16, …

   c 5, 15, 30, 50, 75, …   **d** 4, 6, 9, 13, 18, …

② Investigate how the sequences below relate to the sequence of square numbers. Use this relationship to find the nth term of each sequence.

   a 2, 5, 10, 17, 26, …   **b** 3, 12, 27, 48, 75, …

   c 11, 14, 19, 26, 35, …   **d** 10, 40, 90, 160, 250, …

③ Think of a number.

Follow the instructions on the right.

Prove that no matter what number you started with, you will always end up with 1.

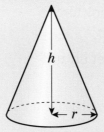

Instructions
Multiply your number by 3.
Add 5.
Double the result.
Subtract 4.
Divide the result by 6.
Subtract the original number.

TASK 6: Deriving formulae

 Points to remember

⊙ When you derive formulae, first represent any unknown quantities with letters.

⊙ You can use formulae that you know to help you to derive new formulae.

⊙ Simplify any results to help you to remember and use them.

Volume V of a cone of radius r and perpendicular height h is:

$$V = \tfrac{1}{3}\pi r^2 h$$

Volume V of a sphere of radius r is:

$$V = \tfrac{4}{3}\pi r^3$$

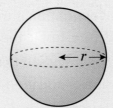

1 In this question, use $\pi \approx 3$.

   a What is the approximate volume of a cone with base radius 5 cm and perpendicular height 15 cm?

   b What is the approximate volume of a cone with base diameter 8 cm and perpendicular height 20 cm?

   c A cone has an approximate volume of 588 cm³ and base radius of 7 cm. Find its perpendicular height.

   d A cone has an approximate volume of 2025 cm³ and perpendicular height of 25 cm. Find its base radius.

2 In this question, use $\pi \approx 3$.

   a Find the approximate volume of a hockey ball with radius 3.6 cm.

   b Find the approximate volume of a basket ball which has diameter 24.4 cm.

   c The approximate volume of a sphere is 500 cm³. What is its radius?

   d The approximate volume of a sphere is 0.5 cm³. What is its diameter?

3 A train leaves a station and travels a distance s for time t with constant acceleration a.

Its final velocity v is given by $v^2 = 2as$.

The distance s is given by $s = \frac{1}{2}at^2$.

Use these two formulae to show that $v = at$.

Trigonometry 1

TASK 1: Pythagoras' theorem in 3D

⊙ Points to remember

- In any right-angled triangle, the **hypotenuse**, the longest side, is opposite the right angle.

- **Pythagoras' theorem** states that in a right-angled triangle the square on the hypotenuse equals the sum of the squares on the other two sides:

$$a^2 + b^2 = c^2$$

- To calculate lengths in 3D shapes, identify right-angled triangles and use Pythagoras' theorem.

Example

The pyramid ABCDO has a rectangular base.
Point O is vertically above M, the centre of the base.
Calculate the length of OM.

First find BD. Using Pythagoras' theorem in triangle BAD:

$$BD^2 = 12^2 + 9^2 = 225$$
$$BD = \sqrt{225} = 15 \, cm$$

Now find OM. Using Pythagoras' theorem in triangle OMB:
BM is $\frac{1}{2}$BD.

$$OM^2 = OB^2 - BM^2 = 18^2 - 7.5^2 = 267.75$$
$$OM = \sqrt{267.75} = \mathbf{16.4 \, cm} \text{ (to 3 s.f.)}$$

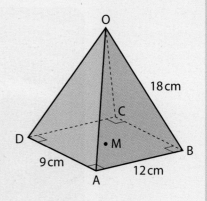

You need a scientific calculator. Give your answers correct to 3 significant figures.

1 Calculate the length AG for these cuboids.

a

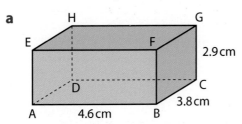

b

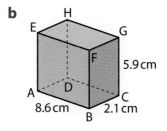

2 ABCDEF is a right-angled triangular prism.
Calculate the length of:

   a BC

   b CD

   c CE

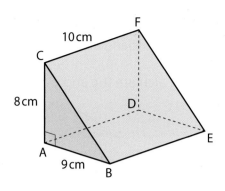

3 The pyramid ABCDE has a square base.
Point E is vertically above O, the centre of the base.
Calculate the length of:

   a AC

   b DE

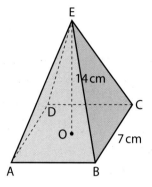

TASK 2: Finding an unknown angle

 Points to remember

⊙ To find an unknown angle of a right-angled triangle, given two sides, choose the ratio that refers to the two sides relative to the unknown angle.

⊙ $\sin^{-1}x$ means the angle whose sine is x,
$\cos^{-1}x$ means the angle whose cosine is x,
$\tan^{-1}x$ means the angle whose tangent is x.

⊙ Give your answer to a suitable degree of accuracy (usually three significant figures for lengths and one decimal place for angles).

Example

Find the size of angle z.

You know the hypotenuse and adjacent side, so use cosine.

$$\cos = \frac{\text{adj}}{\text{hyp}}$$

$$\cos z = \frac{3}{8} = 0.375$$

$$z = \cos^{-1} 0.375 = 68.0 \text{ (to 1 d.p.)}$$

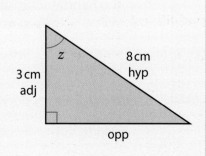

You need a scientific calculator. Give your answers correct to 1 decimal place. Sketch the triangles and show your working.

1 Calculate the angles a, b, c, d, and e in the diagrams below.

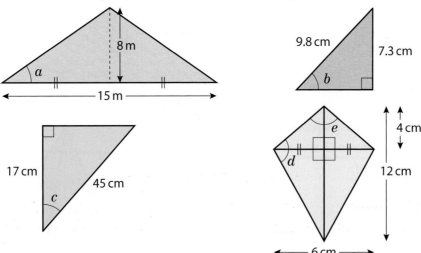

TASK 3: Finding an unknown side

⦿ Points to remember

⊙ The **angle of elevation** is the angle up from the horizontal towards a point.

⊙ The **angle of depression** is the angle down from the horizontal towards a point.

⊙ You can use the trigonometric ratios to find unknown angles and sides in right-angled triangles.

Example

Find the length x.

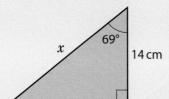

You know the adjacent side and you want to find the hypotenuse, so use cosine.

$$\cos x = \frac{\text{adjacent}}{\text{hypotenuse}}$$

$$\cos 69° = \frac{14}{x}$$

Multiply both sides by x: $x \cos 69° = 14$

Divide both sides by $\cos 69°$:

$$x = \frac{14}{\cos 69°} = \textbf{39.1 cm} \text{ (to 3 s.f.)}$$

You need a scientific calculator. Give your answers correct to 3 significant figures.
You will need to draw a diagram. Remember to show your working.

1 Calculate the lengths a and b.

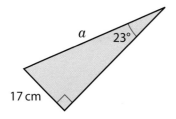

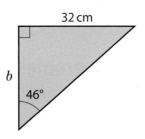

2 The diagram shows a garage with a sloping roof.

Find the length of the sloping roof, c, and the height of the taller side of the garage, d.

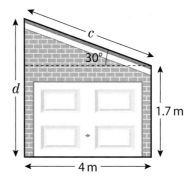

3 In the diagram, XY represents a vertical tower.

A and B are points 30 metres apart at the same horizontal level as the base of the tower.

The angle of elevation of X from A is 30°.
The angle of elevation of X from B is 50°.

Calculate the height of the tower XY in metres.
Give your answer correct to 3 significant figures.

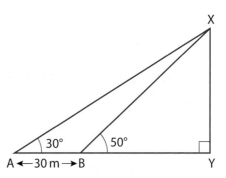

Proportional reasoning

TASK 1: Percentage problems

> **⊙ Points to remember**
>
> ⊙ You can work out percentage increases and decreases, or reverse percentages, using the **unitary method** or **decimal multipliers**.
>
> ⊙ The unitary method involves finding 1% as an intermediate step.
>
> ⊙ **Compound interest** is paid on the original investment plus any previous interest, e.g. for compound interest of 3% for 5 years:
>
> Final amount at end of 5 years = initial amount $\times 1.03^5$
>
> Total interest at the end of 5 years = final amount − initial amount

1. A box of chocolates claims to be 24% bigger.
   It now contains 26 chocolates.
   How many chocolates did it have before the increase?

2. After a 10% discount in price, a weekend break costs £288.
   How much was it before the discount?

3. A digital radio costs £112.80, including 17.5% VAT.
   What did it cost before VAT was added?

4. A pair of designer jeans is on sale at £96, which is 60% of its original price.
   What was the original price?

5. How much would you have in the bank if you had invested £6000 at 4.5% compound interest per annum for 7 years?

6. Shares can decrease in value as well as increase. How much would your shares be worth if you had invested £750, which lost 5.2% each year for 5 years?

7. 65.4% of the population of Qatar is male.
   18.9% of the male population and 34% of the female population are under the age of 15. What percentage of the total population is under 15?

8. A shop marks up the price on a pair of designer jeans to make a profit of 45%.
   In a sale, the shop offers a discount of 15% off the marked price.
   The designer jeans are sold in the sale.
   What percentage profit does the shop make on the jeans?

TASK 2: Direct proportion 1

 Points to remember

⊙ Two quantities y and x are **directly proportional** if their ratio $y : x$ stays the same as the quantities increase or decrease.

⊙ $y \propto x$ (y is directly proportional to x) can be written as $y = kx$, where k is the constant of proportionality.

⊙ The graph of the relationship between two variables that are directly proportional is a straight line through the origin.

⊙ You can use the **unitary method** to solve direct proportion problems by reducing the value of one of the variables to 1.

⊙ When you solve problems involving direct proportion:
  – make sure that corresponding quantities are in the same units;
  – ask yourself whether the answer should be larger or smaller than the quantity already given.

You need some graph paper.

1 y is directly proportional to x.

  a $y = 2$ when $x = 4$. Find y when $x = 10$.

  b $y = 1$ when $x = 5$. Find y when $x = 8$.

2 An air conditioning unit uses 16 units of electricity in 5 hours.
Its use of electricity is directly proportional to the time it is running.
How much electricity will the air conditioner use in 7 hours?

3 A satellite covers a distance of 22 000 km in 4 hours 10 minutes.
The distance travelled is directly proportional to the time taken.
Calculate the time taken to travel 27 000 km.

4 The height, h mm, of a stack of cards is directly proportional to the number of cards, n, in the stack.

When $n = 50$, $h = 28$.

  a Find a formula for h in terms of n.

  b Find the value of h when $n = 60$.

  c Find the value of n when $h = 98$.

(5) The height of a sunflower grown from seed is measured to the nearest centimetre every week for 5 weeks. The results are shown in the table.

Week	1	2	3	4	5
Height (cm)	23	46	69	92	115

a Plot the points on a graph and join them with a suitable line.

b Is the growth in centimetres directly proportional to the time in weeks?

c Write down the equation of the line showing the relationship between the height, h, of the sunflower and the number of weeks, n, it has been growing.

d If the sunflower continued to grow at the same rate, after how many weeks would it first reach a height over 2 metres?

TASK 3: Direct proportion 2

 Points to remember

- $y \propto x^2$ (y is directly proportional to the square of x) can be written as $y = kx^2$, where k is constant.
- $y \propto x^3$ (y is directly proportional to the cube of x) can be written as $y = kx^3$, where k is constant.
- The graph of $y = kx^2$ is a **quadratic curve** passing through the origin.

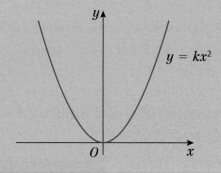

(1) y is directly proportional to the square of x.

    a $y = 8$ when $x = 2$. Find y when $x = 3$.   **b** $y = 12$ when $x = 5$. Find y when $x = 10$.

(2) p is directly proportional to the cube of q.

    a $p = 250$ when $q = 5$. Find p when $q = 2$. **b** $p = 8$ when $q = 4$. Find p when $q = 3$.

3 a is directly proportional to the square of b.

When $a = 80$, $b = 4$.

a Express a in terms of b.

b Work out the value of a when $b = 7$.

c Work out the positive value of b when $a = 45$.

4 A shape is made from identical cubes.
The surface area, $A\,\text{cm}^2$, of the shape is proportional to the square of the edge of the cube, $x\,\text{cm}$.

When $A = 350$, $x = 5$.

a Write a formula for A in terms of x.

b Find the value of A when $x = 8$.

c Find the value of x when $A = 1200$.

5 The mass, m grams, of a candlestick is directly proportional to the cube of its height, $h\,\text{cm}^3$.

When $m = 80\,\text{g}$, $h = 10\,\text{cm}$.

a Write a formula for m in terms of h.

b Find the mass of a candlestick of height 15 cm.

c What is the height of a candlestick weighing 150 g?
Give your answer to three significant figures.

TASK 4: Inverse proportion

 Points to remember

⊙ Two quantities a and b are **inversely proportional** if a increases as b decreases at the same rate, so their product is constant.

⊙ If y is inversely proportional to x, then $y = \dfrac{k}{x}$, where k is a constant.

⊙ If y is inversely proportional to x^2, then $y = \dfrac{k}{x^2}$, and $x = \dfrac{\sqrt{k}}{\sqrt{y}}$, so x is inversely proportional to $\sqrt{y}$.

⊙ When you solve word problems involving inverse proportion, ask yourself if the answer should be larger or smaller than the quantity already given.

Graph of $y = \dfrac{k}{x}$, $k > 0$

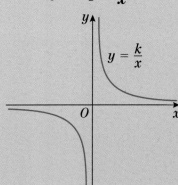

$y = \dfrac{k}{x}$

Graph of $y = \dfrac{k}{x^2}$, $k > 0$

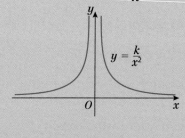

$y = \dfrac{k}{x^2}$

① A shelf is filled with 20 books, each 3.5 cm thick.
The books are replaced by 28 books of equal thickness, which also fill the shelf.
How thick are these books?

② Seven men can pack 2352 boxes of apples in 4 hours.
How long would it take five men to pack 3150 boxes of apples?

③ p is inversely proportional to q.
When $q = 10$, $p = 12$.

   a Write a formula for p in terms of q.

   b Find the value of p when $q = 20$.

   c Find the value of q when $p = 25$.

④ The force, F newtons, between two magnets is inversely proportional
to the square of the distance, d cm, between them.
When $d = 2$, $F = 12$.

   a Write an expression for F in terms of d.

   b Calculate F when $d = 4$.

   c Calculate d when $F = 192$.

⑤ The shutter speed S of a camera varies inversely as
the square of the aperture setting f.
When $f = 8$, $S = 125$.

   a Write a formula for S in terms of f.

   b Calculate the value of S when $f = 4$.

   c Sketch a graph to show the relationship
between S and f.

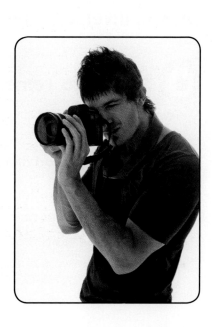

TASK 5: Proportion and square roots

 Points to remember

- $y \propto \sqrt{x}$ (y is directly proportional to $\sqrt{x}$) can be written as $y = k\sqrt{x}$, where k is a constant.

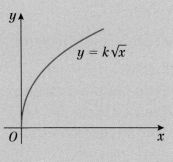

- $y \propto \dfrac{1}{\sqrt{x}}$ (y is inversely proportional to $\sqrt{x}$) can be written as $y = \dfrac{k}{\sqrt{x}}$, where k is a constant.

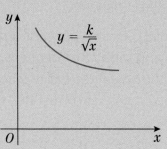

1 y is directly proportional to the square root of x.

   a $y = 12$ when $x = 4$.
     i Find y when $x = 25$.
     ii Find x when $y = 42$.

   b $y = 21$ when $x = 49$.
     i Find y when $x = 121$.
     ii Find x when $y = 27$.

2 p is inversely proportional to the square root of m.

   a $p = 50$ when $m = 15$.
     i Find p when $m = 25$.
     ii Find m when $p = 10$.

   b $p = \frac{1}{2}$ when $m = 4$.
     i Find p when $m = 16$.
     ii Find m when $p = 2$.

3 Here are three examples of proportional relationships.

- d is directly proportional to t.
- V is directly proportional to the cube of r.
- t is inversely proportional to the square root of s.

For each example:

   a write the relationship as a formula, using k for the constant of proportionality

   b draw a sketch of the graph to represent the relationship.

4 When a ball is thrown upwards, the time, t seconds, the ball takes to go up and down again is directly proportional to the square root of the height reached by the ball, h metres.

When $h = 4$, $t = 7$.

a Write a formula for t in terms of h.

b A ball is thrown upwards.
It reaches a height of 10 metres.
How long is it in the air?
Give your answer correct to
3 significant figures.

c The ball is thrown upwards again.
It stays in the air for 5 seconds.
Find the height the ball reaches.
Give your answer correct to 3 significant figures.

Geometrical reasoning

TASK 1: Tangents and chords

Points to remember

⊙ The **tangent** at a point on a circle is perpendicular to the radius at the point.

⊙ The tangents to a circle from a point outside the circle are equal in length.

⊙ The perpendicular from the centre of a circle to a **chord** bisects the chord.

⊙ The line joining the midpoint of a chord to the centre of the circle is perpendicular to the chord.

The diagrams are not drawn accurately.

1   O is the centre of each circle. Calculate the size of each angle marked with a letter. Explain your answer, giving reasons.

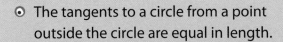

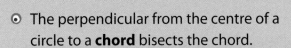

2 PA and PB are tangents to a circle, centre O. Find the sizes of angle x and angle y. Explain your answers, giving reasons.

a

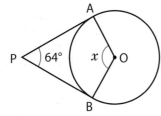

b

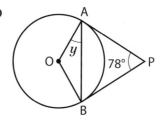

TASK 2: Circle theorems

 Points to remember

⊙ The **angle at the centre of a circle** is twice the angle at the circumference, so $b = 2a$.

⊙ The **angle in a semicircle** is a right angle.

⊙ **Angles in the same segment** are equal.

The diagrams are not drawn accurately.

1 Calculate the size of each angle marked with a letter. Explain your answers, giving reasons.

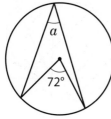

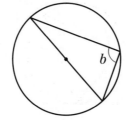

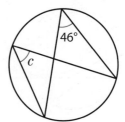

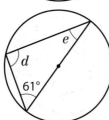

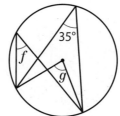

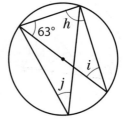

(2) In each circle, AOB is a diameter.
Calculate angle ABP, giving your reasons.

a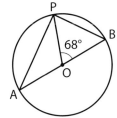

b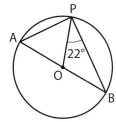

c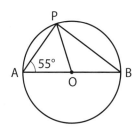

TASK 3: More circle theorems

 Points to remember

⊙ When four points A, B, C and D lie on the
circumference of a circle then ABCD is a
cyclic quadrilateral.

⊙ The sum of the opposite angles of a cyclic
quadrilateral is 180°, so:

$a + c = 180°$, and $b + d = 180°$

⊙ The angle between a tangent and a chord is equal
to the angle in the **alternate segment**.
This is called the **alternate segment theorem**.

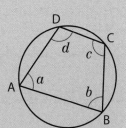

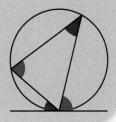

The diagrams are not drawn accurately.

(1) Calculate the size of each angle marked with a letter. Explain your answers, giving reasons.

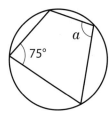

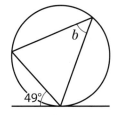

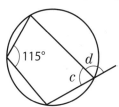

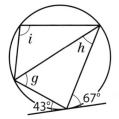

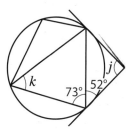

2 The diagram shows a circle with centre O.

ABCD is a cyclic quadrilateral.
Angle BAC = 43° and angle CAD = 47°.

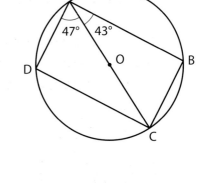

  a Write down the size of angle ACB.

  b Explain why ABCD is a rectangle.

  c Explain why BD is a diameter of the circle.

  d Explain why all rectangles are cyclic quadrilaterals.

3 PA is a tangent to the circle at A.
AB is a diameter of the circle.

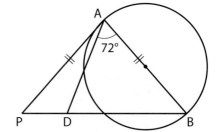

D is a point on PB such that angle BAD = 72°.

AP = AB

Calculate the size of angle PDA.

TASK 4: Using the circle theorems

 Points to remember

⊙ Once a fact has been proved, it can be used to prove further facts.

⊙ These facts can be used to solve problems involving angles in circles:
  – The angle at the centre of a circle is twice the angle at the circumference.
  – The angle in a semicircle is a right angle.
  – Angles in the same segment are equal.
  – The sum of the opposite angles of a cyclic quadrilateral is 180°.
  – The tangent at a point on a circle is perpendicular to the radius at the point.
  – Tangents to a circle from a point outside the circle are equal in length.
  – The perpendicular from the centre to a chord bisects the chord.
  – The angle between the tangent and a chord is equal to the angle in the alternate segment.

The diagrams are not drawn accurately.

1. O is the centre of each circle.
   A, B, C and D are points on the circumference.
   Calculate the size of each angle marked with a letter. Explain your answers, giving reasons.

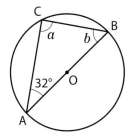 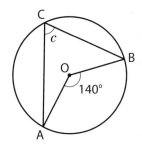 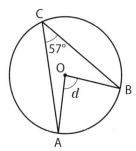

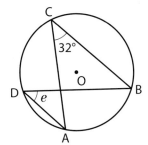 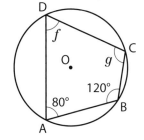 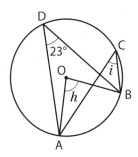

2. In these circles O is the centre.
   A, B and C are points on the circumference.
   PAQ is a tangent.
   Calculate the size of each angle marked with a letter. Show your working.

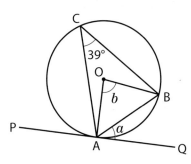 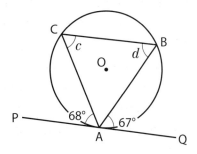

3. The diagram shows a circle with centre O.
   A, B and C are points on the circumference.
   TAP and TBQ are tangents.
   Angle ATB = 70° and angle PAC = 54°.

   Calculate the angles marked a and b.
   Give reasons for each step in your working.

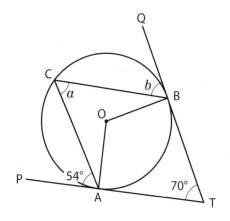

TASK 5: Congruent triangles

⦿ Points to remember

⊙ Two or more shapes are **congruent** if they are the same shape and size.

⊙ Triangles are congruent if they satisfy one of these conditions:

SSS Corresponding sides are equal.

SAS Two sides and the angle between them are equal.

ASA Two angles and a corresponding side are equal.

RHS A right angle, the hypotenuse and one other side are equal.

The diagrams are not drawn accurately.

1 Which two of these triangles are congruent? Give a reason for your answer.

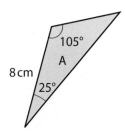 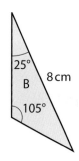 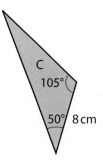 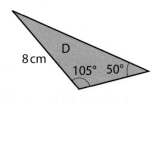

2 Which two of triangles A, B, C, D and E are congruent to triangle T? Give a reason for your answer.

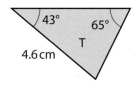

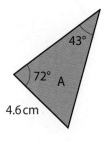 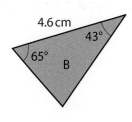 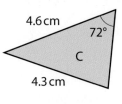

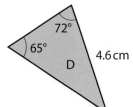 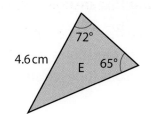

TASK 6: Proving congruency

Points to remember

⊙ To prove that two triangles are **congruent**, show that one of these conditions is satisfied:

SSS   Corresponding sides are equal.

SAS   Two sides and the angle between them are equal.

ASA   Two angles and a corresponding side are equal.

RHS   A right angle, the hypotenuse and one other side are equal.

⊙ You can use congruent triangles to prove that the standard constructions work.

The diagrams are not drawn accurately.

1   A, B, C and D are points on the circumference of a circle with centre O.
AC and BD are diameters of the circle.

Prove that triangle OAB is congruent to triangle OCD.

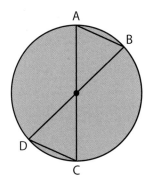

2   ABC is an isosceles triangle.
X is a point on AB and Y is a point on AC.
Angle BCX = angle CBY

Prove that triangle BCX is congruent to triangle CBY.

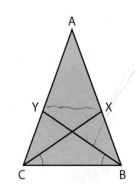

3   ABCD is a regular hexagon.

 a Prove that triangle ABC is congruent to triangle DEF.

 b Prove that triangle ACF is congruent to triangle DFC.

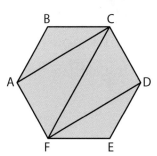

TASK 7: Similar shapes and solids

Points to remember

⊙ In **similar shapes**, lengths of corresponding sides are in the same ratio.

⊙ Regular polygons with the same number of sides are similar.

⊙ All circles are similar and all spheres are similar.

⊙ For similar shapes or solids, when **lengths** are multiplied by k:
  – **areas** are multiplied by k^2;
  – **volumes** are multiplied by k^3.

The diagrams are not drawn accurately.

① State whether each of the pairs of triangles below are similar or not.

a

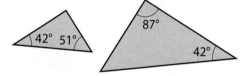

b

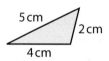

c

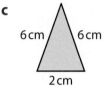

d

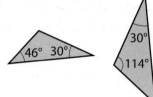

② In triangle ABC, DE is parallel to BC. Find the length of BC.

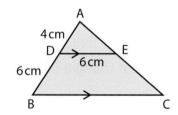

③ Shapes ABCD and EFGH are mathematically similar.

  a Calculate the length of BC.

  b Calculate the length of EF.

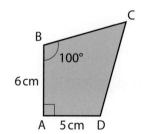

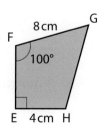

4 Cylinder **A** and cylinder **B** are mathematically similar.

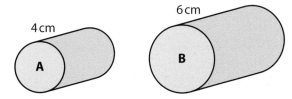

The length of cylinder **A** is 4 cm.
The length of cylinder **B** is 6 cm.
The volume of cylinder **A** is 80 cm³.
Calculate the volume of cylinder **B**.

5 Two cuboids, **S** and **T**, are mathematically similar.

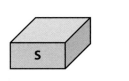 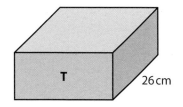

The total surface area of cuboid **S** is 157 cm².
The total surface area of cuboid **T** is 2512 cm².

a The length of cuboid **T** is 26 cm.
Calculate the length of cuboid **S**.

b The volume of cuboid **S** is 130 cm³.
Calculate the volume of cuboid **T**.

Probability 1

TASK 1: Using tree diagrams

⊙ Points to remember

- **Mutually exclusive outcomes** are outcomes that cannot occur at the same time.
- Two events are **independent** when the outcomes of one event do not affect the outcomes of the other event.
- You can use **tree diagrams** to represent outcomes of combined independent events.
- When A and B are outcomes of independent events:
  P(A and B) = P(A) × P(B).

1 An experiment is carried out on two boxes of counters.

Box X contains
3 red counters and
1 blue counter.

Box Y contains
1 red counter and
4 blue counters.

A counter is picked at random from box X.
Another counter is picked at random from box Y.

a Explain why picking a counter from box X and picking a counter from box Y are independent events.

b Copy and complete this tree diagram to show all the outcomes of the trial.

c Use the tree diagram to work out:

  i P(**R** and **R**)

  ii P(**R** and **B**)

  iii P(**B** and **R**)

  iv P(**B** and **B**)

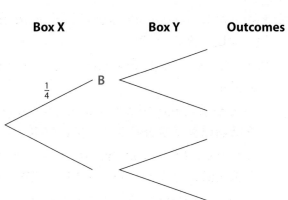

② A box of counters contains 2 red counters and 3 blue counters.

A counter is picked at random from the box.
The counter is replaced and a second counter is picked at random.

   a Explain why the first pick and the second pick from the box are independent events.

   b Draw a tree diagram to show all the possible outcomes.

   c Use the tree diagram to work out:

     i P(**R** and **R**)   **ii** P(**R** and **B**)   **iii** P(**B** and **R**)   **iv** P(**B** and **B**)

③ An experiment is carried out on two boxes of counters.

Box A contains 1 red counter, Box B contains 1 red counter
1 blue counter and 2 green and 1 green counter.
counters.

A counter is picked at random from box A.
A counter is picked at random from box B.

   a Draw a tree diagram to show all the possible outcomes.

   b Use the tree diagram to work out:

     i P(**R** and **R**)   **ii** P(**G** and **G**)   **iii** P(**B** and **R**)

     iv P(**B** and **G**)   **v** P(**R** and **G**)   **vi** P(**G** and **R**)

TASK 2: The probability of combined events

◉ Points to remember

⊙ When outcomes A and B of an event are mutually exclusive:
P(A or B) = P(A) + P(B).

⊙ For two combined independent events each with mutually exclusive outcomes **A** and **B**:

  – The probability that the outcomes are the same is:
    P(**A** and **A** or **B** and **B**) = P(**A**) × P(**A**) + P(**B**) × P(**B**)

  – The probability that the outcomes are different is:
    P(**A** and **B** or **B** and **A**) = P(**A**) × P(**B**) + P(**B**) × P(**A**)

  – The probability of at least one A is:
    P(**A** and **A** or **A** and **B** or **B** and **A**) = P(**A**) × P(**A**) + P(**A**) × P(**B**) + P(**B**) × P(**A**)
    or 1 − P(**B** and **B**) = 1 − P(**B**) × P(**B**)

1 Look at questions 1 and 2 from Task 1.

For each question work out:

 a P(both counters are the same colour)

 b P(the counters are different colours)

 c P(at least one red counter is picked)

2 The arrow on this fair spinner is spun twice.

The colours that the arrow lands on are recorded for each spin.

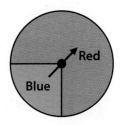

 a Copy and complete this tree diagram to show all the possible outcomes.

 b Use the tree diagram to work out the probability that the colours obtained are the same.

1st spin   **2nd spin**   **Outcome**

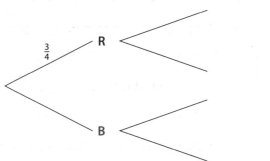

3 Tim spins the arrow on this fair spinner twice.

He writes down the numbers the arrow lands on and adds them to obtain a score.

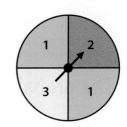

 a Copy and complete this tree diagram to show all the possible scores that Tim can score.

 b Use the tree diagram to work out the probability that Tim scores 4.

First spin   **Second spin**   **Total**

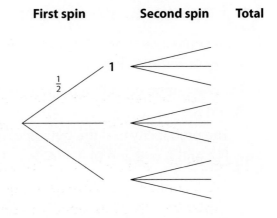

TASK 3: Investigating a game of chance

  Points to remember

- Relative frequency and theoretical probability can be compared to investigate whether or not a simple game is a game of chance.
- You can use probability theory to investigate strategies for playing a game of chance.

① Two players play Rock, paper, scissors.

Player 1 chooses rock, paper and scissors in the ratio 3 : 2 : 1.
Player 2 chooses rock, paper and scissors in the ratio 3 : 2 : 5.

a Write down the probability that Player 1 chooses:

   i rock   **ii** paper   **iii** scissors

b Write down the probability that Player 2 chooses:

   i rock   **ii** paper   **iii** scissors

c Copy and complete this tree diagram to show all the outcomes of a game between Player 1 and Player 2.

Player 1	Player 2	Outcome	Result
	R	R and R	A tie
R	P	R and P	Player 2

d Use the tree diagram to work out the probability that:

   i Player 1 wins   **ii** Player 2 wins   **iii** the game is a tie.

② In a Rock, paper, scissors match you notice that your opponent chooses scissors about once in every five hand signals.
Apart from that your opponent seems equally likely to choose rock and paper.

What is your best strategy for winning the game?
Justify your answer by working out appropriate probabilities.

TASK 4: Conditional probability

Points to remember

⊙ When the outcomes of an event depend on the outcomes of a previous event, the events are not independent.

⊙ The probability of an outcome of an event that depends on the outcome of a previous event is called **conditional probability**.

⊙ You can use tree diagrams to help work out conditional probabilities.

1. The tree diagram shows the outcomes and probabilities of two events.

   a. Explain why the tree diagram shows that the events are **not** independent.

   b. Work out P(**A** and **A** *or* **B** and **B**).

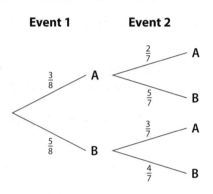

2. Mark has two 20 pence coins and three 10 pence coins in his pocket. He takes two coins from his pocket at random.

   a. Copy and complete this tree diagram to show all the possible outcomes. Write the probabilities of each outcome on the branches of the tree diagram.

   b. Calculate the probability that Mark has 40 pence left in his pocket. Show your working.

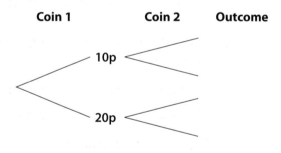

3. In any week, the probability that Ali is late for school on a Monday is $\frac{1}{4}$.

   If he is late on Monday the probability that he is late for school on Tuesday is $\frac{2}{5}$.
   If he is **not** late on Monday the probability that he is late for school on Tuesday is $\frac{1}{10}$.

   a. Draw a tree diagram to show whether Ali is late or **not** late for school on a Monday and a Tuesday in any week.
   Write the probabilities of each outcome on the branches of the diagram.

   b. Estimate the number of times that Ali is **not** late on both a Monday and a Tuesday in a school year of 40 weeks.

   c. Work out the probability that Ali is late on either a Monday or Tuesday of a school week.

TASK 5: The 'and' and 'or' rules

 Points to remember

⊙ You can use the **'and' and 'or' rules** for combined events (independent and not independent) to solve probability problems without a tree diagram.

1 The probability that Tim is late for work on Monday is 0.4.
The probability that he is late for work on Tuesday is 0.3.

What is the probability that he will be late for work next Monday and Tuesday?

2 Jane rolls a fair six-sided 1–6 dice.
Bill rolls a fair four-sided 1–4 dice.

  a The numbers that both dice land on are added.

    i Work out the probability of a total of 10.

    ii Work out the probability of a total of 8.

  b Work out these probabilities.

    i Jane's dice and Bill's dice land on the same number.

    ii One dice lands on a number that is double the number on the other dice.

3 The probability that a hockey team wins its next match is:

  ⊙ 0.4 if they won their last match;

  ⊙ 0.7 if they lost their last match.

  a The team loses a match.

    What is the probability that they will win the next two matches?

  b The team wins a match.

    What is the probability that they will win the next two matches?

A
7.3

Solving equations

TASK 1: Linear equations

◉ Points to remember

- Before you solve a **linear equation**, simplify expressions on both sides.
- If there are algebraic fractions in the equation, multiply through by the lowest common denominator.
- Rearrange the equation to get the unknown on one side and numbers on the other.
- There are often different ways of approaching solutions to equations. Look carefully at the equation and try to find the most efficient method.

(1) Solve the equations.

   a $2(5x - 16) - 3(2x + 4) = 4$ **b** $4(3x - 2) + 3(5x + 4) = 11(2x + 4)$

   c $\dfrac{3x}{4} + \dfrac{7x}{10} = 29$ **d** $\dfrac{19x}{9} - \dfrac{7x}{12} = 55$

(2) Solve the equations.

   a $\dfrac{7x + 11}{9} + \dfrac{6x + 5}{13} = 14$ **b** $\dfrac{3x + 4}{5} - \dfrac{2x - 5}{3} = 2$

   c $\dfrac{x}{8} + 2 = \dfrac{x}{16} + 4$ **d** $\dfrac{9x}{4} + 5 = \dfrac{5x}{2} - 4$

TASK 2: Solving quadratic equations graphically

◉ Points to remember

- A **quadratic graph** may cut the x-axis at two points, touch it at one point or not touch it at all.
- At any point (x, y) where the graph of $y = ax^2 + bx + c$ meets the x-axis:
  - the value of y is 0;
  - the value of x is a solution of the equation $ax^2 + bx + c = 0$.
- A **quadratic equation** has two real solutions, one real solution or no real solution.

You need some graph paper.

1 Write the equation of the graph you would draw to help you solve these equations.

   a $x^2 + 3x - 70 = 0$

   b $x^2 - 3x = 28$

   c $x^2 - 5x - 16 = 50$

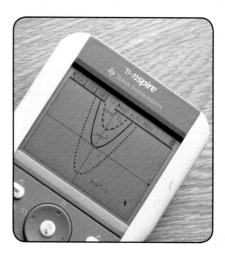

2 Draw graphs to solve these equations. Check your answers by substituting each value for x back into the original equation.

   a $x^2 + 2x - 35 = 0$

   b $x^2 + x = 56$

   c $x^2 - 8x + 4 = 24$

TASK 3: Solving quadratic equations by factorisation 1

> **⊙ Points to remember**
>
> ⊙ To solve a quadratic equation by **factorisation**:
> - factorise the quadratic expression;
> - in turn, make each bracket equal zero and find the value of x;
> - check the solutions by substituting the values into the original equation.

Example

Solve $x^2 + x - 6 = 0$.

$x^2 + x - 6 = 0 \equiv (x + 3)(x - 2)$	First factorise the left-hand side.
When $(x + 3)(x - 2) = 0$, either $(x + 3) = 0$ or $(x - 2) = 0$.	Make each factor equal to zero.
If $(x + 3) = 0$, then $x = -3$. If $(x - 2) = 0$, then $x = 2$.	Solve each equation.
The solutions of $x^2 + x - 6 = 0$ are $x = -3$ **and** $x = 2$.	Write the answer.
When $x = -3$, $(-3)^2 - 3 - 6 = 0$ When $x = 2$, $(2)^2 + 2 - 6 = 0$	Check by substituting each value back into the original equation.

1 Use factorisation to solve these quadratic equations.
Check your answers by substituting each value for x back into the original equation.

   a $x^2 + x - 2 = 0$ **b** $x^2 - 3x + 2 = 0$ **c** $x^2 - x - 2 = 0$

2 Use the method of factorisation to solve these quadratic equations.
Check your answers by substituting each value for x back into the original equation.

   a $x^2 - 9x + 20 = 0$ **b** $x^2 + 7x - 18 = 0$ **c** $x^2 - 2x - 35 = 0$

   d $x^2 + 11x + 30 = 0$ **e** $x^2 - x - 42 = 0$ **f** $x^2 - 14x + 40 = 0$

   g $x^2 + 11x + 28 = 0$ **h** $x^2 - 16x + 63 = 0$ **i** $x^2 - 8x - 40 = 7x + 14$

TASK 4: Solving quadratic equations by factorisation 2

Points to remember

○ To solve a quadratic equation by **factorisation**:

  – factorise the quadratic expression;

  – in turn, make each bracket equal to zero and find the value of x;

  – check the solutions by substituting the values back into the
    original equation.

Example

Solve $10x^2 + 3x - 1 = 0$.

$10x^2 + 3x - 1 \equiv (2x + 1)(5x - 1)$ First factorise the left-hand side.

When $(2x + 1)(5x - 1) = 0$, then   Make each factor equal to zero.
either $(2x + 1) = 0$ or $(5x - 1) = 0$.

If $(2x + 1) = 0$, then $x = -0.5$.   Solve each equation.
If $(5x - 1) = 0$, then $x = 0.2$.

The solutions of $10x^2 + 3x - 1 = 0$ are   Write the answer.
$x = -0.5$ and $x = 0.2$

When $x = -0.5$, $10 \times 0.25 - 1.5 - 1 = 0$ Check by substituting each value
When $x = 0.2$, $10 \times 0.04 + 0.6 - 1 = 0$ back into the original equation.

1 Use factorisation to solve these quadratic equations.

   a $6x^2 + 7x - 20 = 0$ **b** $12x^2 + 13x - 14 = 0$ **c** $25x^2 - 9 = 0$

   d $6x^2 + 11x - 2 = 0$ **e** $8x^2 - 6x + 1 = 0$ **f** $9x^2 + 12x + 4 = 0$

   g $8x^2 + 11x + 3 = 0$ **h** $7x^2 - 5x - 2 = 0$ **i** $5x^2 - 12x = 6x - 9$

TASK 5: Completing the square

> ### ● Points to remember
> ⊙ The solutions of $x^2 = p$ are $x = \pm\sqrt{p}$.
> ⊙ The solutions of $(x + a)^2 = q$ are:
> $$x + a = \pm\sqrt{q}$$
> giving $\quad\quad x = -a \pm\sqrt{q}$
> ⊙ You can rearrange a quadratic equation in the form $(x + a)^2 = q$ to solve it.

1 Find two values of x to satisfy these equations.

  a $(x - 2)^2 = 1$ **b** $(x + 8)^2 = 36$

  c $(x - 7)^2 = 16$ **d** $(x - 5)^2 = 81$

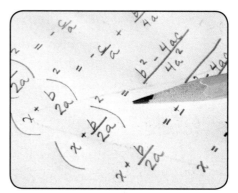

2 Find two values of x to satisfy these equations. Give your answers to 3 significant figures.

  a $(x - 10)^2 = 40$ **b** $(x + 4)^2 = 78$

  c $(x - 3)^2 = 19$ **d** $(x - 11)^2 = 29$

3 Find two values of x that satisfy these equations. Give your answers to 3 significant figures.

  a $(x - 7)^2 - 43 = 20$ **b** $(x - 7)^2 + 18 = 76$ **c** $(x + 5)^2 + 9 = 31$

  d $(x - 9)^2 - 5 = 45$ **e** $(x + 3)^2 - 12 = 64$ **f** $(x - 11)^2 - 10 = 19$

TASK 6: Using the quadratic formula

> ### ● Points to remember
> ⊙ The **formula for solving any quadratic equation** $ax^2 + bx + c = 0$ is
> $$x = \frac{-b \pm \sqrt{b^2 - 4ac}}{2a}.$$
> ⊙ Memorise the formula by saying 'minus b plus or minus the square root of b squared minus four ac all over two a'.

1 Solve these quadratic equations by using the formula. Give answers to three significant figures.

  a $x^2 - 3x + 1 = 0$ **b** $x^2 + 8x - 5 = 0$ **c** $x^2 + 5x - 13 = 0$

  d $x^2 + 7x + 1 = 0$ **e** $x^2 + 9x + 2 = 0$ **f** $x^2 - 10x + 7 = 0$

2 Solve these quadratic equations by using the formula. Give answers to three decimal places.

a $3x^2 - 7x - 2 = 0$ **b** $5x^2 + 2x - 4 = 0$ **c** $2x^2 - x - 7 = 0$

d $2x^2 + 5x - 1 = 0$ **e** $4x^2 + 6x - 3 = 0$ **f** $8x^2 - x - 3 = 0$

TASK 7: Simultaneous linear and quadratic equations

● Points to remember

◉ The simultaneous solutions to **one linear and one quadratic equation** are where their graphs intersect.

◉ To solve a pair of **simultaneous equations, one linear and one quadratic**, using an algebraic method:
  – make one variable the subject of the linear equation;
  – substitute for this variable into the quadratic equation, and solve it using factorisation or the formula;
  – in turn, substitute each value back into the linear equation and find the corresponding value of the other variable.

Example

Solve $y = x^2 - 2$ ....(1)

                         $y = x + 4$ ....(2)

(1) − (2) $0 = x^2 - x - 6$

Factorise $0 = (x - 3)(x + 2)$

                         $x = 3$ or $x = -2$

Substitute for x in (2) $y = 7$ or $y = 2$

The solutions are $x = \mathbf{3}, y = \mathbf{7}$ and $x = \mathbf{-2}, y = \mathbf{2}$.

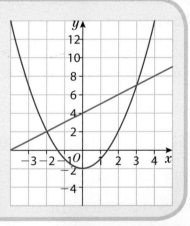

1 Solve these pairs of simultaneous equations.

a $y = x^2 + 3x + 1$
    $y = x + 4$

b $y = x^2 + 2x + 1$
    $y = x + 1$

c $y = 2x^2 + x - 4$
    $y = -x$

d $y = 3x^2 + 2x - 5$
    $y = -4x - 5$

2 Solve these pairs of simultaneous equations.

a $y - x + 1 = x^2$
$y + 3x = 4$

b $y - 2x - x^2 + 2 = 0$
$y - 3x = 10$

c $y + x^2 + 3x = 6$
$y - 2x = 6$

d $y + x^2 + 4x = 10$
$4x - y + 17 = 0$

TASK 8: Simultaneous linear and non-linear equations

 Points to remember

⊙ To solve a pair of **simultaneous equations, one linear and one non-linear**, using an algebraic method:
  – make one variable the subject of the linear equation;
  – substitute for this variable into the non-linear equation, and solve it;
  – in turn, substitute each value back into the linear equation and find the corresponding value of the other variable.

⊙ When you find the solution to a linear and non-linear equation it is useful to sketch a graph first. This helps you to check solutions.

1 Solve these simultaneous equations.
Give your answers to 3 significant figures.

a $y = x^2 + 2x - 2$
$y = -x + 1$

b $y = x^2 - 3x - 1$
$y = -x + 3$

c $y = -x^2 + 5x + 3$
$y = x - 3$

2 Solve these simultaneous equations.
Give your answers to 3 significant figures.

a $x^2 + y^2 + 2x = 25$
$y = 2x + 2$

b $xy = 10$
$y = 3x + 1$

c $x^2 + 2y^2 = 20$
$y = 2x$

Transformations and vectors

TASK 1: Symmetry patterns

◉ Points to remember

- An **isometry** of the plane is a transformation in the plane that preserves length and therefore shape. The four isometries are translations, reflections, rotations and **glide reflections**.

- There are three categories of symmetry patterns: **rosette patterns** (two types), **frieze patterns** (seven types) and **wallpaper patterns** (17 types).

- Geometrical patterns play an important part in architecture and art.

- Every culture has a preference for certain types of symmetry patterns. The important thing is not the motif in the patterns, but the types of symmetry. This can be used to date objects and identify connections between different cultures.

① Continue your research into symmetry patterns and write up your notes. Prepare to present your findings in the form of an illustrated magazine article.

② Read the article 'Frieze patterns in cast iron' by Heather McLeay. You can find this on the NRICH website at:
nrich.maths.org/public/viewer.php?obj_id=1341

TASK 3: Vectors and vector notation

Points to remember

⊙ A **vector** has magnitude and direction.

⊙ This vector can be written as $\overrightarrow{AB}$ or **a** or as $\begin{pmatrix} 3 \\ 4 \end{pmatrix}$.

⊙ A **displacement** is a change in position.

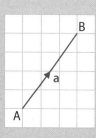

You need some squared paper.

1 A ferry sails from A to B.

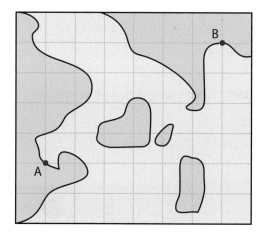

a The first part of the journey is represented by the column vector $\begin{pmatrix} 2 \\ 2 \end{pmatrix}$.

Plan a route for the rest of the journey then write column vectors to represent it.

b Write the column vectors for the reverse journey by the same route.

c On a second occasion, the first two stages of the journey are $\begin{pmatrix} 1 \\ 1 \end{pmatrix}$ followed by $\begin{pmatrix} 3 \\ -3 \end{pmatrix}$.

d Plan a route for the rest of the journey then write column vectors to represent it.

2 On squared paper, plot the points A (2, 5), B (5, 8), C (3, −5) and D (−6, 4).

Now write as column vectors:

   a $\overrightarrow{AD}$ **b** $\overrightarrow{AC}$ **c** $\overrightarrow{BD}$ **d** $\overrightarrow{CA}$ **e** $\overrightarrow{CD}$ **f** $\overrightarrow{BC}$

3 Y is the point (5, 9) and $XY = \begin{pmatrix} -4 \\ 6 \end{pmatrix}$. What are the coordinates of X?

TASK 4: The magnitude of a vector

Points to remember

⊙ The magnitude of the vector $\overrightarrow{AB}$ is AB, which is the distance from A to B.

⊙ The magnitude of the vector **p** is written as p.

⊙ The magnitude of the vector $\begin{pmatrix} a \\ b \end{pmatrix}$ is the positive value of $\sqrt{a^2 + b^2}$.

⊙ The magnitudes of $\begin{pmatrix} a \\ b \end{pmatrix}$ and $\begin{pmatrix} -a \\ -b \end{pmatrix}$ are equal.

⊙ $-\overrightarrow{AB} = \overrightarrow{BA}$

⊙ Two vectors are equal only if they have the same magnitude and the same direction; vectors with the same magnitude are not necessarily equal.

⊙ Lines with the same direction are parallel; lines that are parallel can have opposite directions.

① Work out the magnitude of each vector. Where necessary, leave your answer as a surd.

a $\begin{pmatrix} 15 \\ 20 \end{pmatrix}$ b $\begin{pmatrix} 3 \\ -21 \end{pmatrix}$ c $\begin{pmatrix} -18 \\ 27 \end{pmatrix}$ d $\begin{pmatrix} -12 \\ -35 \end{pmatrix}$ e $\begin{pmatrix} -75 \\ 100 \end{pmatrix}$ f $\begin{pmatrix} 20 \\ 21 \end{pmatrix}$

② Zola rides her bike from home.
She goes 2 km north and then 3 km west and then another 2 km north.

a Write column vectors to show her movements.

b How far is Zola from home 'as the crow flies'?

c What is Zola's bearing from her starting point?

③ In triangle ABC, $\overrightarrow{AB} = \begin{pmatrix} 13 \\ -84 \end{pmatrix}$ and $\overrightarrow{AC} = \begin{pmatrix} -36 \\ -77 \end{pmatrix}$.

Show that triangle ABC is isosceles.

④ WXYZ is a quadrilateral. $\overrightarrow{WX} = \begin{pmatrix} 5 \\ 6 \end{pmatrix}$, $\overrightarrow{XY} = \begin{pmatrix} 8 \\ 0 \end{pmatrix}$ and $\overrightarrow{YZ} = \begin{pmatrix} -5 \\ -6 \end{pmatrix}$

a What type of quadrilateral is WXYZ?

b What is its area?

c What is the length of WY? You may leave your answer as a surd.

TASK 5: Vector addition

Points to remember

- $\overrightarrow{AB} + \overrightarrow{BC} = \overrightarrow{AC}$ refers to vectors or displacements, not to distances.
- $\overrightarrow{AC}$ is the **resultant** of $\overrightarrow{AB} + \overrightarrow{BC}$.
- $\begin{pmatrix} a \\ b \end{pmatrix} + \begin{pmatrix} c \\ d \end{pmatrix} = \begin{pmatrix} a + c \\ b + d \end{pmatrix}$
- $\mathbf{a} - \mathbf{b} = \mathbf{a} + (-\mathbf{b})$
- The vector $\overrightarrow{AB}$ can be expressed as the sum of several vectors if the end of one vector is the start of the next, so $\overrightarrow{AB} = \overrightarrow{AC} + \overrightarrow{CD} + \overrightarrow{DE} + \overrightarrow{EB}$.

You need plain paper, a ruler and protractor.

1 Find these vector sums.

a $\begin{pmatrix} 2 \\ -3 \end{pmatrix} + \begin{pmatrix} 1 \\ 6 \end{pmatrix}$ **b** $\begin{pmatrix} -2 \\ 3 \end{pmatrix} + \begin{pmatrix} -1 \\ -7 \end{pmatrix}$ **c** $\begin{pmatrix} 6 \\ 0 \end{pmatrix} + \begin{pmatrix} -8 \\ 2 \end{pmatrix}$

d $\begin{pmatrix} 1 \\ 5 \end{pmatrix} + \begin{pmatrix} -4 \\ -5 \end{pmatrix}$ **e** $\begin{pmatrix} -1 \\ -4 \end{pmatrix} + \begin{pmatrix} -4 \\ 8 \end{pmatrix}$

2 A vector **x** has magnitude 5 cm and direction 330°.
A vector **y** has magnitude 4 cm and direction 90°.
Draw and label the vectors:

     a **x**   **b** **y**   **c** −**y**   **d** **x** + **y**   **e** **x** − **y**

3 Make scale drawings to find the magnitude and direction of the resultant of each pair of vectors:

     a a wind of 8 m/s in an easterly direction and a yacht's velocity of 12 m/s north east

     b a force of 25 newtons vertically and a force of 10 newtons at 20° below the horizontal.

TASK 6: Parallel vectors and problem solving

 Points to remember

- A quantity with magnitude but no direction is called a **scalar**.
- When $\overrightarrow{AB} = k\overrightarrow{CD}$, where k is a positive scalar, the lines AB and CD are parallel and the length of AB is k times the length of CD.
- When $\overrightarrow{AB} = k\overrightarrow{AE}$, the points A, B and E lie on the same straight line.
- $k\begin{pmatrix} a \\ b \end{pmatrix} = \begin{pmatrix} ka \\ kb \end{pmatrix}$, where k is a scalar.
- The **position vector** of the point P is the vector $\overrightarrow{OP}$, where O is the origin.
- You can use vectors to solve geometric problems.

① $\mathbf{p} = \begin{pmatrix} 3 \\ 5 \end{pmatrix}$ and $\mathbf{q} = \begin{pmatrix} -2 \\ 4 \end{pmatrix}$. Find:

   a $2\mathbf{p}$ **b** $3\mathbf{q}$ **c** $3\mathbf{p} + 4\mathbf{q}$ **d** $5\mathbf{p} - 2\mathbf{q}$

② The points X, Y and Z have coordinates (1, 12), (3, 20) and (5, 28) respectively.

   Write $\overrightarrow{XY}$ and $\overrightarrow{XZ}$ as column vectors.

   What do these show about the points X, Y and Z?

③ OAB is a triangle.

   P divides the line AB in the ratio $1:4$.

   $\overrightarrow{OA} = \mathbf{a}$ and $\overrightarrow{OB} = \mathbf{b}$.

   Write $\overrightarrow{BP}$ in terms of $\mathbf{a}$ and $\mathbf{b}$.

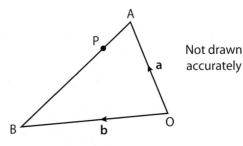

Not drawn accurately

④ PQRS is a quadrilateral where $\overrightarrow{PQ} = \mathbf{p}$, $\overrightarrow{QR} = \mathbf{q}$, $\overrightarrow{RS} = \mathbf{r}$ and $\overrightarrow{PS} = 3\mathbf{q}$.

   a What type of quadrilateral is PQRS?

   b Express $\mathbf{r}$ in terms of $\mathbf{p}$ and $\mathbf{q}$.

⑤ The vector $\begin{pmatrix} 2 \\ 4 \end{pmatrix}$ is one side of an isosceles triangle.

   Which of these vectors could be one of the other sides of the triangle?

$$\begin{pmatrix} 4 \\ 0 \end{pmatrix} \quad \begin{pmatrix} 0 \\ 4 \end{pmatrix} \quad \begin{pmatrix} 6 \\ 0 \end{pmatrix} \quad \begin{pmatrix} 0 \\ 6 \end{pmatrix} \quad \begin{pmatrix} 8 \\ 0 \end{pmatrix} \quad \begin{pmatrix} 0 \\ 8 \end{pmatrix} \quad \begin{pmatrix} 1 \\ 3 \end{pmatrix} \quad \begin{pmatrix} -1 \\ 3 \end{pmatrix}$$

Enquiry 2

TASK 1: Sampling and statistics

 Points to remember

⊙ Each sample from a population is different and will produce different results.

⊙ Smaller samples tend to be more variable.

⊙ Larger samples are more similar to each other and to the whole population.

The mode, median and mean are different ways of finding the average of a set of numbers. The range shows how spread out the numbers are.

▢ The **mode** is the number that occurs most often in the set.

▢ The **mean** is the sum of all the numbers divided by the number of numbers.

▢ The **median** is the middle number, or the mean of the middle two numbers, when all the numbers are arranged in order.

▢ The **range** is the difference between the highest and lowest numbers.

① Use a scientific calculator to generate some sets of random numbers. Generate eight samples each of 15 numbers between 1 and 20.

   a For each sample, write down the mean, median and range.

   b For each sample, what is the longest unbroken run of one number?

   c Describe the variability in your samples.

TASK 2: Five-figure summaries

 Points to remember

⊙ The **five-figure summary** for a set of data is given by the minimum, lower quartile, median, upper quartile and maximum.

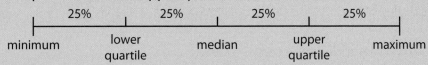

⊙ The **interquartile range** is a measure of the spread over the middle 50% of the data and is the difference between the upper and lower quartiles.

Example

Work out the five-figure summary and the interquartile range for the average temperatures in Cairo in the table below.

Month	Jan	Feb	Mar	Apr	May	Jun	Jul	Aug	Sep	Oct	Nov	Dec
Temp (°C)	12.4	13.9	16.9	20.8	24.4	27.2	28.1	27.8	25.2	22.8	18.5	14.4

First order the data: 12.4, 13.9, 14.4, 16.9, 18.5, 20.8, 22.8, 24.4, 25.2, 27.2, 27.8, 28.1

Next find the median: the middle pair is 20.8 and 22.8 so the median temperature is 21.8°C.

Now find the median for the lower half of the data: 12.4, 13.9, 14.4, 16.9, 18.5, 20.8
The middle pair is 14.4 and 16.9 so the lower quartile temperature is 15.65°C.

Now find the median for the upper half of the data: 22.8, 24.4, 25.2, 27.2, 27.8, 28.1
The middle pair is 25.2 and 27.2 so the upper quartile is 26.2°C.

The five-figure summary is 12.4°C, 15.65°C, 21.8°C, 26.2°C, 28.1°C.

The interquartile range is $26.2 - 15.65 = 10.55°C$.

1 Work out the five-figure summary and the interquartile range for these sets of data.

  a Average 24-hour temperature in Paris

Month	Jan	Feb	Mar	Apr	May	Jun	Jul	Aug	Sep	Oct	Nov	Dec
Temp (°C)	3.5	4.9	6.9	10.4	13.6	17.3	18.7	18.1	16.2	12.3	7.2	3.5

  b Average rainfall in Paris

Month	Jan	Feb	Mar	Apr	May	Jun	Jul	Aug	Sep	Oct	Nov	Dec
Rain (mm)	182	121	158	205	323	301	237	193	66	63	83	155

  c Average 24-hour temperature in Jakarta, Indonesia

Month	Jan	Feb	Mar	Apr	May	Jun	Jul	Aug	Sep	Oct	Nov	Dec
Temp (°C)	25.9	26.1	26.6	26.9	27.3	26.8	26.5	26.7	27.1	27.6	27.3	26.6

  d Average rainfall in Jakarta, Indonesia

Month	Jan	Feb	Mar	Apr	May	Jun	Jul	Aug	Sep	Oct	Nov	Dec
Rain (mm)	417	319	212	113	88	62	39	48	34	68	96	16

All data from www.worldclimate.com

2 Use the five-figure summaries and interquartile ranges to compare the weather in the two cities.

TASK 3: Cumulative frequency 1

Points to remember

⊙ The **cumulative frequency** at a particular point is the 'running total' of all the frequencies up to that point.

⊙ You can represent cumulative frequencies in a **cumulative frequency table** and plot them on a **cumulative frequency graph**.

Example

The cumulative frequency table shows information about the times in minutes 30 patients waited at a doctor's surgery. The cumulative frequency column is created from the frequency column. The data is used to produce the cumulative frequency graph.

Time (minutes)	Frequency	Cumulative frequency
$0 < t \leq 5$	1	1
$5 < t \leq 10$	5	$1 + 5 = 6$
$10 < t \leq 15$	12	$6 + 12 = 18$
$15 < t \leq 20$	10	$18 + 10 = 28$
$20 < t \leq 25$	2	$28 + 2 = 30$

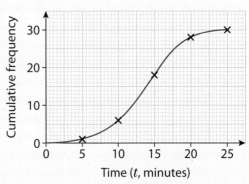

You need some graph paper.

1. The grouped frequency table gives information about the finish times of the competitors in the Great Langdale Christmas Pudding 10 km race in 2007 (data: www.thepowerof10.info).

Times (hours:min)	Frequency
$00{:}30 < x \leq 00{:}40$	74
$00{:}40 < x \leq 00{:}50$	171
$00{:}50 < x \leq 01{:}00$	166
$01{:}00 < x \leq 01{:}10$	38
$01{:}10 < x \leq 01{:}20$	3
$01{:}20 < x \leq 01{:}30$	1

a Draw a cumulative frequency table and graph for the data.

b Use your graph to estimate how many runners finished in 1 hour 15 minutes or less.

c Use your graph to estimate how many runners had a finishing time of 45 minutes or less.

d Estimate how many runners had a finishing time of from 50 to 55 minutes.

TASK 4: Cumulative frequency 2

Points to remember

⊙ You can use a cumulative frequency graph to estimate the median, lower quartile and upper quartile for a large data set containing n values:
- use the value at $\frac{1}{2}n$ for the **median**;
- use the value at $\frac{1}{4}n$ for the **lower quartile**;
- use the value at $\frac{3}{4}n$ for the **upper quartile**.

The cumulative frequency graph shows the times 80 pupils took to answer a mental mathematics question.

Use the graph to estimate:

$\frac{3}{4}$ of 80 = 60
start at 60

a the lower quartile

3.2

$\frac{1}{2}$ of 80 = 40
start at 40

b the upper quartile

4.1

c the interquartile range

$\frac{1}{4}$ of 80 = 20
start at 20

4.1 − 3.2 = 0.9

d the median

3.6

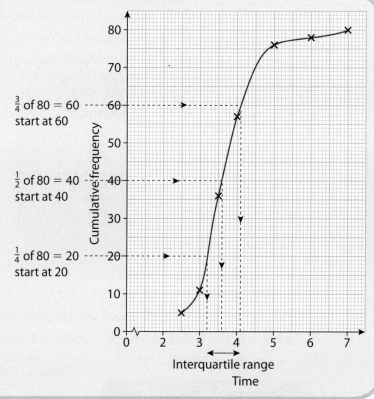

You need graph paper.

① The grouped frequency table shows information on the time taken by 100 pupils to complete a test.

a Draw a cumulative frequency table for the data.

b Use the table to draw the cumulative frequency graph.

c Use your graph to estimate the median, upper quartile, lower quartile and interquartile range for the data.

Time (min)	Frequency
$20 < x \leqslant 22$	7
$22 < x \leqslant 24$	9
$24 < x \leqslant 26$	35
$26 < x \leqslant 28$	41
$28 < x \leqslant 30$	4
$30 < x \leqslant 32$	3
$32 < x \leqslant 34$	1

2 This grouped frequency table shows the times taken by 120 pupils to travel to school.

Time (min)	Frequency
$0 < x \leqslant 5$	5
$5 < x \leqslant 10$	18
$10 < x \leqslant 15$	36
$15 < x \leqslant 20$	41
$20 < x \leqslant 25$	15
$25 < x \leqslant 30$	5

a Draw a cumulative frequency table for the data.

b Draw the cumulative frequency graph.

c Use your graph to estimate the median, upper quartile, lower quartile and interquartile range for the data.

TASK 5: Estimating statistics for grouped data

 Points to remember

⊙ When data is grouped, you cannot calculate accurate values of average and spread but you can estimate them.

⊙ You can calculate an **estimate of the mean** from a grouped frequency table using this formula:

$$\frac{\Sigma(f \times x)}{\Sigma f}$$

where: the symbol Σ means 'the sum of'

x represents the midpoint of the class interval

f represents the frequency of the class.

Example

The table shows the maximum daily temperature in Fort Nelson in Canada for 90 days in summer 2007.

The source of the data is:
www.climate.weatheroffice.ec.gc.ca

Estimate the mean maximum daily temperature.

Temperature (°C)	Frequency
$10 < x \leqslant 15$	7
$15 < x \leqslant 20$	30
$20 < x \leqslant 25$	35
$25 < x \leqslant 30$	16
$30 < x \leqslant 35$	2

Assume that the mean of the values in each class interval is at the **midpoint** of the class interval.

Temperature (°C)	Midpoint of interval	Frequency	Midpoint × frequency
$10 < x \leqslant 15$	12.5	7	87.5
$15 < x \leqslant 20$	17.5	30	525
$20 < x \leqslant 25$	22.5	35	787.5
$25 < x \leqslant 30$	27.5	16	440
$30 < x \leqslant 35$	32.5	2	65

Work out frequency (the number of values) × midpoint of class and add them together.

Estimated total of temperatures = 1905   Number of days = 90

Estimated mean maximum daily temperature = 1905 ÷ 90 = 21.2°C

1 This table shows the maximum and minimum daily temperatures for Fort Nelson in Canada for the whole of 2007.

a Calculate an estimate for the mean maximum daily temperature.

b Calculate an estimate for the mean minimum daily temperature.

Temperature (°C)	Frequency maximum daily temperature	Frequency minimum daily temperature
$-35 < x \leqslant -30$	0	10
$-30 < x \leqslant -25$	1	22
$-25 < x \leqslant -20$	13	50
$-20 < x \leqslant -15$	42	27
$-15 < x \leqslant -10$	36	33
$-10 < x \leqslant -5$	26	17
$-5 < x \leqslant 0$	23	55
$0 < x \leqslant 5$	30	54
$5 < x \leqslant 10$	28	44
$10 < x \leqslant 15$	45	46
$15 < x \leqslant 20$	54	7
$20 < x \leqslant 25$	44	0
$25 < x \leqslant 30$	19	0
$30 < x \leqslant 35$	4	0

Source: www.climate.weatheroffice.ec.gc.ca/Welcome_e.html

TASK 6: Box plots

⊙ Points to remember

⊙ A **box plot** should always be drawn to scale.

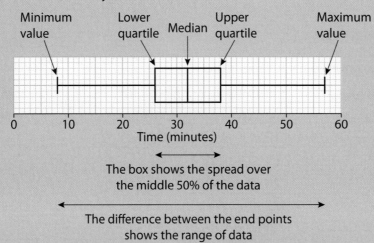

The box shows the spread over the middle 50% of the data

The difference between the end points shows the range of data

⊙ You can use box plots to compare distributions. Draw one box plot above the other using the same scale or a shared scale.

You need some graph paper.

1 A class took four different tests.
Each test was out of 100 marks.
The summary statistics for the test
are shown in the table.

a Draw a box plot for each test,
one above the other, using the
same scale.

b Compare the distributions of the
test scores using the box plots.

	Test 1	Test 2	Test 3	Test 4
Minimum	20	5	60	30
Lower quartile	40	10	74	40
Median	50	20	80	65
Upper quartile	60	30	90	70
Maximum	80	50	100	90

TASK 7: Histograms and frequency density

 Points to remember

⊙ When a **histogram** has unequal class intervals, the area of each rectangle
is proportional to the frequency.

⊙ The vertical axis is labelled '**frequency density**'.

⊙ The height of each rectangle is the frequency density of the class, where:

$$\textbf{frequency density} = \frac{\text{frequency}}{\text{class width}}$$

Example

The table gives some information about the distance
that a number of people threw a ball.

Draw a histogram to represent the data.

Distance (m)	Frequency
$0 < x \leqslant 10$	10
$10 < x \leqslant 20$	100
$20 < x \leqslant 30$	70
$30 < x \leqslant 45$	30
$45 < x \leqslant 70$	25

First calculate the class widths. Next, find the frequency
densities by dividing the frequency by the class width.

Distance (m)	Frequency	Class width	Frequency density = frequency ÷ class width
$0 < x \leqslant 10$	10	10	$10 \div 10 = 1$
$10 < x \leqslant 20$	100	10	$100 \div 10 = 10$
$20 < x \leqslant 30$	70	10	$70 \div 10 = 7$
$30 < x \leqslant 45$	30	15	$30 \div 15 = 2$
$45 < x \leqslant 70$	25	25	$25 \div 25 = 1$

The histogram shows the data in the table. Because the intervals are unequal, frequency density is plotted on the vertical axis.

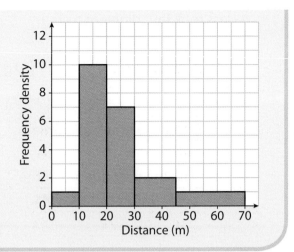

You need some graph paper.

1. The table shows information about the weights of some melons grown on a farm.

   Draw a histogram to represent the data.

Melon weight (kg)	Frequency
$0 < x \leqslant 1.5$	5
$1.5 < x \leqslant 2.0$	9
$2.0 < x \leqslant 2.5$	16
$2.5 < x \leqslant 3.0$	15
$3.0 < x \leqslant 4.0$	4

2. The table shows information about the weights of some strawberries grown on a farm.

   Draw a histogram to represent the data.

Strawberry weight (g)	Frequency
$10 < x \leqslant 15$	10
$15 < x \leqslant 20$	16
$20 < x \leqslant 22$	32
$22 < x \leqslant 24$	46
$24 < x \leqslant 26$	54
$26 < x \leqslant 28$	38
$28 < x \leqslant 30$	28
$30 < x \leqslant 35$	6

TASK 8: Moving averages

◉ Points to remember

- ⊙ Some time series data sets show regular patterns called **seasonality**, peaking at certain points in the year on a regular cycle.
- ⊙ To look for trends and patterns in the data over time, plot the **moving averages**.
- ⊙ Draw a **trend line** as the line of best fit and use it to make predictions for the future based on past performance.

Example

The table shows the quarterly sales of racing bicycles made by a company.

Quarter	Year 1	Year 2	Year 3
1	67	74	54
2	190	201	254
3	117	121	131
4	246	321	344

Calculate the first three 4-point moving averages.

The mean of the first 4 values (Q1, Q2, Q3, Q4 of year 1) is:

$(67 + 190 + 117 + 246) \div 4 = 155$ bicycles

The mean of the next 4 values (Q2, Q3, Q4 of year 1 and Q1 of year 2) = 157 bicycles

The mean of the next 4 values (Q3, Q4 of year 1 and Q1, Q2 of year 2) = 160 bicycles

You need some graph paper.

1. The table gives some information about the number of marriages quarterly in England and Wales (data from www.statistics.gov.uk).

Year	Quarter			
	1	2	3	4
2000	31 492	74 194	116 695	45 580
2001	28 836	70 876	105 331	44 184
2002	31 893	71 124	105 671	46 908
2003	34 025	75 152	111 869	49 063

a Draw a time series graph to represent the data in the table.

b Calculate the 4-point moving averages for the data.

c Plot the moving averages on your graph.

d Is there a seasonal pattern to weddings?

e Is marriage becoming more popular or less popular in England and Wales? Give reasons for your answer.

Trigonometry 2

TASK 1: 2D and 3D problems

⦿ Points to remember

- ⊙ By identifying right-angled triangles in 2D figures and 3D shapes, you can use **Pythagoras' theorem** and **trigonometry** to find:
  - – angles and lengths of sides of triangles;
  - – the angle between a line and a plane.
- ⊙ Do not round numbers until the final answer.
- ⊙ In answers, unless specified, give lengths to 3 significant figures and angles to 1 decimal place.

1. The diagram shows a piece of square paper with the corners cut off to leave a rectangle.

   The total area of the four shaded triangles is 200 cm².

   What is the length of the diagonal of the rectangle?

   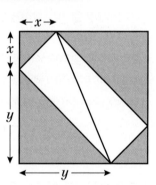

2. PQRSTU is a triangular prism.

   In triangle PQR, angle RPQ = 90°, PQ = 12 cm and PR = 15 cm.

   In rectangle PQST, the length of QT = 8 cm.

   Calculate the size of the angle between:

   a   RQ and PQTS

   b   RS and PQTS

   c   RT and PQTS

   d   QR and PSUR.

   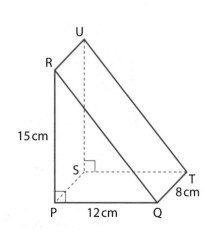

TASK 2: Area of a triangle

Points to remember

⊙ The **area of triangle ABC is** $\frac{1}{2}ab\sin C$
or 'half the product of two sides times
the sine of the included angle'.

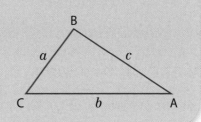

You need a scientific calculator.

1 Calculate the area of each triangle.

a
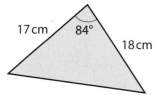
17 cm 84° 18 cm

b
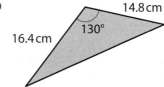
14.8 cm 130° 16.4 cm

2 Calculate the lengths a and b.

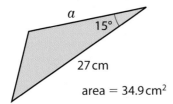
a 15° 27 cm area = 34.9 cm²

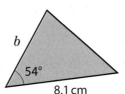
b 54° 8.1 cm area = 19.7 cm²

3 Calculate the sizes of angles x and y.

a
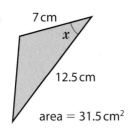
7 cm x 12.5 cm area = 31.5 cm²

b
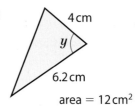
4 cm y 6.2 cm area = 12 cm²

4 Calculate the areas of the quadrilaterals.

a
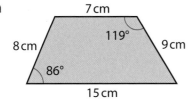
7 cm 119° 9 cm 8 cm 86° 15 cm

b
9 cm 65° 14 cm

TASK 3: Angles larger than 90°

Points to remember

⊙ Trigonometric ratios can be found for angles of any size.

⊙ Graphs can be drawn for $y = \sin x$, $y = \cos x$ and $y = \tan x$.

The diagram shows the graphs of $y = \sin x$ in blue and $y = \cos x$ in red for $0° \leqslant x \leqslant 360°$.

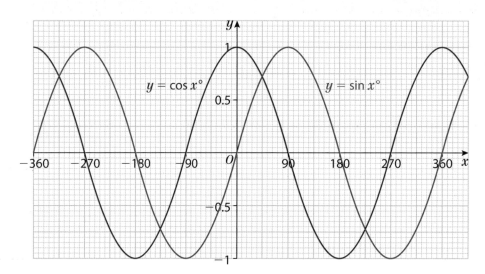

Use the graph to help you to answer the following questions:

1　**a** What is similar about the graphs for
$y = \sin x$ and $y = \cos x$?

　　b What is different about them?

　　c Describe the relationship between them.

2　For what ranges of values of x in the interval $-360° \leqslant x \leqslant 360°$ is:

　　a $\sin x$ positive?　　　　　　　**b** $\sin x$ negative?

　　c $\cos x$ positive?　　　　　　　**d** $\cos x$ negative?

3　Estimate the solutions in the interval $-360° \leqslant x \leqslant 360°$ of:

　　a $\sin x = \cos x$

　　b $\cos x = 0.5$

TASK 4: Graphs of trigonometric functions

 Points to remember

⊙ $\tan x = \dfrac{\sin x}{\cos x}$

⊙ Trigonometric functions are periodic.

⊙ Trigonometric graphs can be transformed by using constants.

⊙ Different trigonometric functions are positive in different quadrants.

Sin +ve	All +ve
sin +	sin +
cos −	cos +
tan −	tan +
sin −	sin −
cos −	cos +
tan +	tan −
Tan +ve	Cos +ve

You need some graph paper and a scientific calculator.

1 a Copy this table of values for $y = 2\sin 3x$ for values of x from $-180°$ to $180°$.

x	$-180°$	$-135°$	$-90°$	$-45°$	$0°$	$45°$	$90°$	$135°$	$180°$
y									

Use your calculator to help you to complete the table.

b Sketch the graph of $y = 2\sin 3x$ for values of x from $-180°$ to $180°$.

c What is the repeating period of the graph of $y = 2\sin 3x$?

d What are the maximum and minimum values of $y = 2\sin 3x$ for $-180° \leqslant x \leqslant 180°$?

2 a Copy this table of values for $y = 2\cos\frac{1}{2}x$ for values of x from $-360°$ to $360°$.

x	$-360°$	$-270°$	$-180°$	$-90°$	$0°$	$90°$	$180°$	$270°$	$360°$
y									

Use your calculator to help you to complete the table.

b Sketch the graph of $y = 2\cos\frac{1}{2}x$ for values of x from $-180°$ to $180°$.

c What is the repeating period of the graph of $y = 2\cos\frac{1}{2}x$?

d What are the maximum and minimum values of $y = 2\cos\frac{1}{2}x$ for $-360° \leqslant x \leqslant 360°$?

TASK 5: The sine rule

  Points to remember

- You can use the **sine rule** to find lengths and
  angles in triangles that are not right-angled:

$$\frac{a}{\sin A} = \frac{b}{\sin B} = \frac{c}{\sin C}$$

$$\frac{\sin A}{a} = \frac{\sin B}{b} = \frac{\sin C}{c}$$

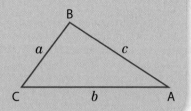

Example 1

Find the length x. Give your answer to 3 significant figures.

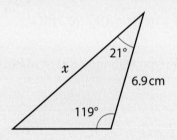

First use the angle sum of a triangle to find the angle
opposite 6.5 cm.

Missing angle $= 180° - 21° - 119° = 40°$

Using the sine rule:

$$\frac{x}{\sin 119°} = \frac{6.9}{\sin 40°}$$

$$x = \frac{6.9 \times \sin 119°}{\sin 40°}$$

$$x = 9.39 \text{ cm (to 3 s.f.)}$$

Example 2

Calculate the acute angle A. Give your answer to 1 decimal place.

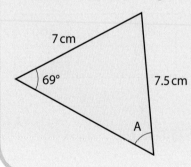

Using the sine rule:

$$\frac{\sin A}{7} = \frac{\sin 69°}{7.5}$$

$$\sin A = \frac{7 \times \sin 69°}{7.5} = 0.8713$$

$$A = \sin^{-1} 0.8713 = 60.6° \text{ (to 1 d.p.)}$$

You need a scientific calculator.

Give your answers to 3 significant figures for lengths and 1 decimal place for angles.

Remember to draw a diagram for each question and to show your working clearly.

1 Find the lengths of the sides of the triangles marked with a letter.

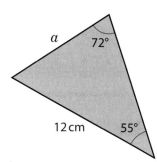

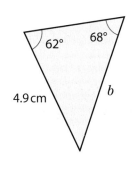

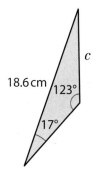

2 Calculate the sizes of the angles marked with a letter.

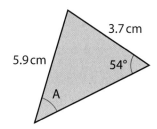

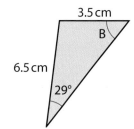

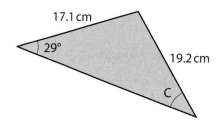

TASK 6: The cosine rule

◉ Points to remember

⊙ You can use the **cosine rule** to find lengths and angles in triangles that are not right-angled:

$$a^2 = b^2 + c^2 - 2bc \cos A$$

$$\cos A = \frac{b^2 + c^2 - a^2}{2bc}$$

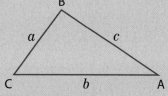

Example 1

Find the length x. Give your answer to 3 significant figures.

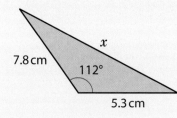

Using the cosine rule:

$$a^2 = b^2 + c^2 - 2bc \cos A$$

$$x^2 = 7.8^2 + 5.3^2 - 2 \times 7.8 \times 5.3 \times \cos 112°$$

$$= 119.90\ldots$$

$$x = \sqrt{119.90\ldots} = 10.9 \text{ cm (to 3 s.f.)}$$

Example 2

Find angle X. Give your answer to 1 decimal place.

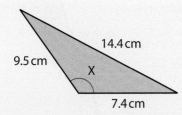

Using the cosine rule:

$$\cos X = \frac{b^2 + c^2 - a^2}{2bc}$$

$$\cos X = \frac{9.5^2 + 7.4^2 - 14.4^2}{2 \times 9.5 \times 7.4}$$

$$= -0.4435$$

The value of cos X is negative so X is an obtuse angle.

$$X = 116.3° \text{ (to 1 d.p.)}$$

You need a scientific calculator.

Give your answers to 3 significant figures for lengths and 1 decimal place for angles.

Remember to draw a diagram for each question and to show your working clearly.

① Find the lengths of the sides marked with letters.

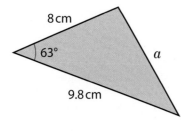

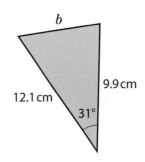

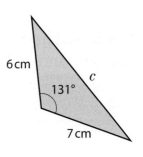

② Calculate the sizes of the angles marked with letters.

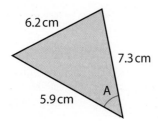

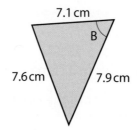

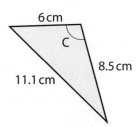

TASK 7: Using the sine and cosine rules

Points to remember

- You can use the **sine and cosine rules** to find lengths and angles in triangles.
- Choose the rule that gives you the answer most directly.
- To **find an angle**:
  - if you know three sides, use the cosine rule;
  - if you know two sides, and an angle opposite one of them, use the sine rule to find the angle opposite the other side.
- To **find a side**:
  - if you know two sides and the included angle, use the cosine rule;
  - if you know two angles, and a side opposite one of them, use the sine rule to find the side opposite the other angle.

Example

Felicity goes orienteering.
She runs 4 km on a bearing of 136°, then 3.5 km on a bearing of 295°.

a How far is Felicity from her starting point?

Draw a diagram and label it to show the route from A to B to C.

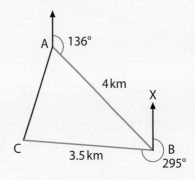

Calculate angle ABC:

Angle ABX = 180° − 136° = 44°
   (angles between parallel lines)

Angle ABC = 360° − 44° − 295° = 21°
   (angles around a point)

Mark these angles on the diagram.

In triangle ABC, use the cosine rule to find CA, the distance from C to the starting point A:

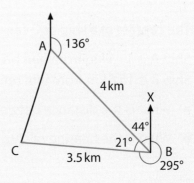

$CA^2 = 4^2 + 3.5^2 - 2 \times 4 \times 3.5 \times \cos 21°$

$CA = 1.45$ km (to 3 s.f.)

So Felicity is **1.45 km** (to 3 s.f.) from A.

b On what bearing must Felicity travel to return directly to her starting point?

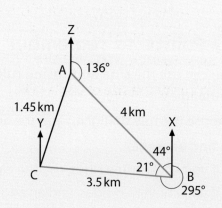

Use the sine rule to calculate angle BAC:

$$\frac{\sin A}{3.5} = \frac{\sin 21°}{1.45}$$

$$\sin A = \frac{3.5 \times \sin 21°}{1.45} = 0.8650...$$

Angle A = $\sin^{-1} 0.8650... = 59.9°$

Angle ZAC = $360° - 136° - 59.9° = 164.1°$
  (angles round a point)

Angle ACY = $180° - 164.1° = 15.9°$ (to 1 d.p.)
  (angles between parallel lines)

So Felicity must travel on a **bearing of 016°** to return from C to A.

You need a scientific calculator.
Give your answers to 3 significant figures for lengths and 1 decimal place for angles.
Remember to draw a diagram for each question and to show your working clearly.

1 Calculate the lengths and angles marked with a letter.

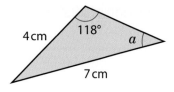

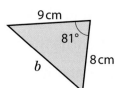

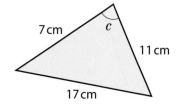

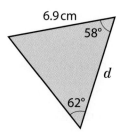

2 The captain of a ship at C can see two other ships.

Ship A is 11.1 km from him on a bearing of 069°.
Ship B is 15.6 km from him on a bearing of 092°.

  a What is the distance between the ships?

  b What is the bearing of ship B from ship A?

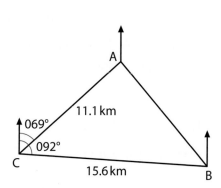

3 The diagram shows a pyramid ABCDE.

The base of the pyramid ABCD is a rectangle with AB = 7 cm and BC = 9.5 cm.

EA = EB = EC = ED = 13 cm

Calculate the size of angle BED.

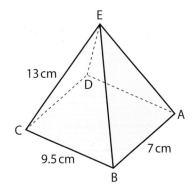

Probability 2

TASK 1: Capture-recapture

> **Points to remember**
>
> ⊙ **Capture-recapture** sampling methods are used to estimate the size of a population when it is impossible count the size exactly.
>
> ⊙ When you choose samples, it is important to consider the assumptions that you make.

1. A biologist set several large traps in a field.
   She caught 150 mice, marked them with non-toxic paint, then released them.
   Four students then set traps to catch a sample of mice.
   Their results are shown in the table.

Student	Captured	Marked
A	180	30
B	160	20
C	205	38
D	110	16

   Which student will report the largest estimate for the population?
   Which will report the smallest?

2. Scientists estimate that the trout population in a mile-long stretch of river is about 2550 trout.
   On their first visit they catch 150 trout. Each fish is tagged, then released.
   On their next visit, they catch 340 trout.
   About how many of the 340 trout will be marked if their estimate of the trout population in the river is a good one?

3. **a** What sort of problems might occur when capture-recapture methods are used?
   b How do you think the size of the samples in a capture-recapture experiment affects the accuracy of the estimate?
   c What other populations could be estimated using a capture-recapture model?

TASK 2: The birthday problem

Points to remember

⊙ For independent or non-independent combined events:
  - you can use tree diagrams to represent outcomes and help work out probabilities;
  - you can use the 'and' and 'or' rules to work out probabilities without a tree diagram.

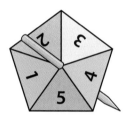

① Armand has two fair spinners.
One has three equal sections labelled A, B and C.
The other has five equal sections numbered from 1 to 5.
He spins the two spinners at the same time.

Calculate the probability of Armand spinning:

a an A and a 1

b a B and an odd number

c an A and a 2 or a C and an even number.

② Felix has a pack of 52 playing cards.
He picks cards from the pack at random one at a time but does not replace them.

Felix picks two cards.
Calculate the probability that he picks:

a a king and a queen

b a red card and a black card

c a number card from 2 to 10 and an ace, king, queen or jack.

Felix then picks a third card.
Calculate the probability that he picks:

d three black cards

e three kings.

TASK 3: Using probability 1

⦿ Points to remember

⊙ You can sometimes use probability to analyse games to work out the chances of winning them and to decide whether or not they are fair.

1 In a game of **Snakes and ladders**, you take turns to throw a fair 1 to 6 dice.

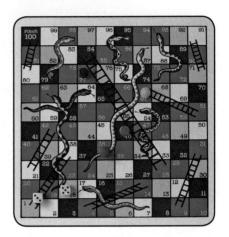

You then move your counter on that number of squares.

If you land at the bottom of a ladder, you climb up to the square at the top.
If you land at the head of a snake, you slide down to the square at the end of its tail.

The first player to land exactly on the winning square wins the game.

A Snakes and ladders board has the numbers 1 to 20 on it.

20	19	18	17	16
11	12	13	14	15
10	9	8	7	6
1	2	3	4	5

a After one throw of the dice, on which number or numbers are you most likely to land? Which number or numbers are least likely?

b After two throws of the dice, on which number or numbers from 2 to 12 are you most likely to land? Which number or numbers are least likely?

c After three throws of the dice, on which number or numbers from 3 to 18 are you most likely to land? Which number or numbers are least likely?

d Design a 1 to 20 Snakes and ladders board to give a fast game.

e Design a 1 to 20 Snakes and ladders board to give a slow game.

TASK 4: Using probability 2

 **Points to remember**

⊙ You can use probability to help you to make decisions and choose good strategies in games of chance and other situations.

 Did you know that...?

Buffon's needle is one of the oldest problems in probability. It was first posed in 1777 by the French scientist **Georges Buffon** (1707−1788), who was important in the field of natural history.

> Given a needle of length l dropped on a sheet of paper ruled with parallel lines l units apart, what is the probability that the needle will cross a line?

Buffon's needle experiment caused much discussion about probability. The unexpected result is that, when the parallel lines are the length of the needle apart, the probability that the needle will land on one of them is $\frac{2}{\pi}$.

You need a piece of plain paper, a ruler, pencil and a cocktail stick or something similar.

1. In this task you are going to try a variation on Buffon's needle problem.

   a Measure the length of your 'needle'.
   Rule your paper with parallel lines the same distance apart as the length of your needle.

   Drop your needle onto your paper 100 times.
   Count how many times it lands across a line.

   Work out the experimental probability that the needle lands across one of the lines.

   b Use the formula **experimental probability** $= \frac{2}{\pi}$ to calculate an estimate for π.
   How close is your estimate?

TASK 5: Quincunx

 Points to remember

⊙ You can solve problems involving probability using the addition and multiplication rules.

⊙ **Pascal's triangle**, in which each number is the sum of the two numbers above it, helps to work out probabilities in the quincunx.

You need your copy of Pascal's triangle on **S7.4 Resource sheet 5.1**.

1 Look at the 'hockey stick' shapes shown in red and blue on the diagram of Pascal's triangle.

    a What do you notice about the numbers?

    b Look at other 'hockey sticks' of different sizes on the grid. Sketch your 'hockey sticks' and describe the relationship between the numbers on them.

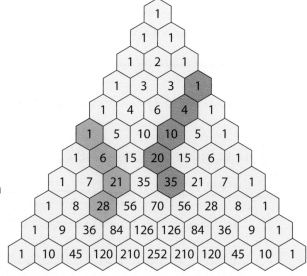

2 If you write the digits in each row as one single number you get this sequence of numbers:

1
11
121
1331
14641

    a What is special about the numbers in the sequence? Does the pattern continue?

    b Write a formula for the nth number in the sequence.

3 In some of the rows of Pascal's triangle, the second number in each row is prime. What do you notice about all the other numbers in those rows?

4   **a** Add up all the numbers on each green diagonal line. What do you notice?

    b What is this sequence called? Explain how it is formed.

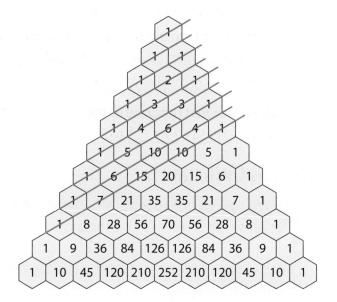

Exploring graphs

TASK 1: Exploring quadratic and cubic functions

⊙ Points to remember

- The **quadratic equation** $y = ax^2 + bx + c$ has a U-shaped graph, which:
  - when a is positive, has a minimum value at its turning point;
  - when a is negative, has a maximum value at its turning point.
- The **cubic equation** $y = ax^3 + bx^2 + cx + d$ has an S-shaped graph, which:
  - when a is positive, starts in the 3rd quadrant and ends in the 1st quadrant;
  - when a is negative, starts in the 2nd quadrant and ends in the 4th quadrant;
  - has two turning points, with one maximum and one minimum value, or no turning points.

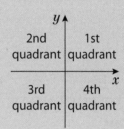

You need graph paper.

1. **a** Without drawing the graph, work out the values of x and y at the minimum point on the graph of $y = x^2 - 2x + 4$.
   Check by sketching the graph.

   b Without drawing the graph, work out the values of x and y at the maximum point on the graph of $y = -x^2 + 4x - 3$.
   Check by sketching the graph.

2. Describe what happens to the gradient of the tangent to the curve $y = -x^2 + 4x + 6$ as x increases from -1 to 5.

3. This is the graph of $y = x^3 - 3x^2 - 2x$.

   Describe what happens to the gradient of the tangent to the curve as x increases from -1 to 4.

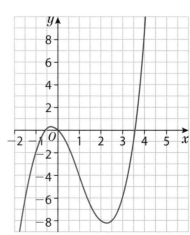

TASK 2: Properties of polynomial functions

Points to remember

- $y = ax + b$, $y = ax^2 + bx + c$, $y = ax^3 + bx^2 + cx + d$ and so on are examples of **polynomial functions**. Each power of x is a positive integer.
- When the highest power is x^n, the polynomial is of **order n**.
- When the order is even, a polynomial graph starts and ends on the same side of the x-axis. It either:
  - starts in the 2nd quadrant and ends in the 1st quadrant; or
  - starts in the 3rd quadrant and ends in the 4th quadrant.
- When the order is odd, a polynomial graph crosses the x-axis at least once. It either:
  - starts in the 3rd quadrant and ends in the 1st quadrant; or
  - starts in the 2nd quadrant and ends in the 4th quadrant.

1. Look at the graph.

   What sort of graph could it be?

   Give your reasons.

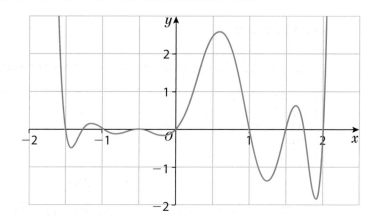

2. Look at the graph.

   What sort of graph could it be?

   Give your reasons.

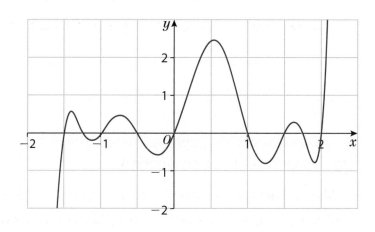

TASK 3: Reciprocal functions

Points to remember

⊙ A **reciprocal function** has an equation of the form $y = \frac{a}{x}$. Its graph:
  - has two parts in diagonally opposite quadrants;
  - does not cross or touch the x-axis or the y-axis;
  - has no maximum or minimum points;
  - is discontinuous, since the function has no value at $x = 0$;
  - approaches the x-axis, without crossing or touching it, at each end.

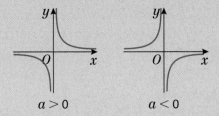

$a > 0$ $a < 0$

You need graph paper.

① **a** Copy and complete the table below for the equation $y = \frac{6}{x}$.

x	−6	−5	−4	−3	−2	−1	1	2	3	4	5	6
y												

b Draw an accurate graph of the equation.

c Describe what happens to y as x increases from −6 to 6.

d Describe what happens to y as x increases beyond 6.

e Describe what happens to y as x decreases from 1 towards zero.

TASK 4: Exponential functions

Points to remember

⊙ When a number is raised to a power, the power is called the **exponent**.

⊙ As the power is increased, so the number increases rapidly.

⊙ The equation $y = a^x$, where a is a constant, represents an **exponential function**.

The **graph of an exponential function**:

⊙ is a continuous curve and is always positive (i.e. above the x-axis);

⊙ crosses the y-axis at (0, 1);

⊙ has no maximum or minimum points;

⊙ increases very rapidly at one end and approaches the x-axis, without crossing or touching it, at the other end.

In general, the graph of $y = a^x$, where a is a positive number, has the same shape as the graph of $y = 2^x$.

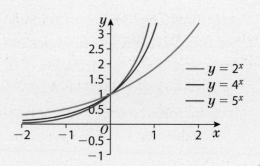

You need some graph paper.

① This sketch shows part of the graph with equation $y = ma^x$, where m and a are positive numbers.

The points with coordinates (1, 6), (3, 24) and (4, k) all lie on the graph.

a Calculate the values of a, m and k.

b Find the coordinates of the point where the graph crosses the y-axis.

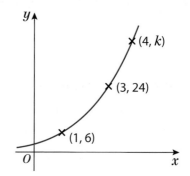

② Draw axes for $-3 \leqslant x \leqslant 3$ and $-3 \leqslant y \leqslant 30$.
On the same axes, sketch the graphs of $y = 3^x$ and $y = 6^x$.
Label each graph clearly with its equation.

③ Write the equation of each graph.

a

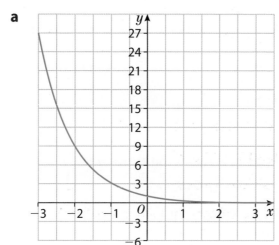

b

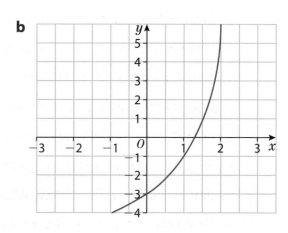

TASK 5: Generating trigonometric functions

Points to remember

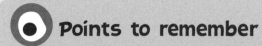

⊙ When a point travelling around a unit circle anticlockwise makes an angle a with the x-axis, its vertical distance from the x-axis is $\sin a$ and its horizontal distance from the y-axis is $\cos a$.

⊙ Plotting the vertical distance against the angle gives a **sine curve**.

⊙ Plotting the horizontal distance against the angle gives a **cosine curve**.

⊙ Trigonometric functions are periodic.

⊙ Different trigonometric functions are positive in different quadrants.

	2nd	1st	
sin	+	sin	+
cos	−	cos	+
tan	−	tan	+

	3rd	4th	
sin	−	sin	−
cos	−	cos	+
tan	+	tan	−

(1) The orange curve is $y = \cos x$. The green curve is $y = \sin x$.

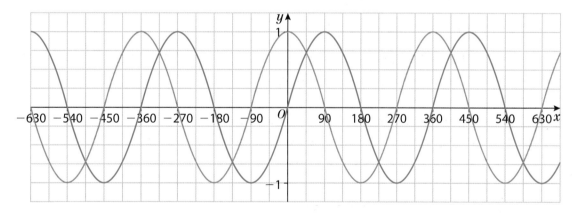

a What is the maximum y-value for $y = \cos x$?

b What is the minimum value for $y = \cos x$?

c Give four values of x where $\cos x = 0$.

d Give four values of x where $\sin x = 0$.

e For what value of x between 0° and 90° does $\cos x = \sin x$?

f Find the value of a in the equation $\sin a = \cos 62°$.

g Find the value of b in the equation $\sin 39° = \cos b$.

h Given that $\cos 25° = 0.906$ (to 3 significant figures), what is $\cos 165°$?

i Explain why $\cos^2 a + \sin^2 a = 1$.

TASK 6: Exploring trigonometric functions

⦿ Points to remember

⊙ Trigonometric graphs are periodic.

⊙ $y = \sin x$ and $y = \cos x$ each have a **period** of 360° and an **amplitude** of 1.

⊙ Trigonometric graphs can be transformed by introducing constants.

① Write the equation, period and amplitude of each graph.

a

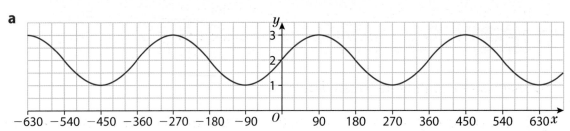

b

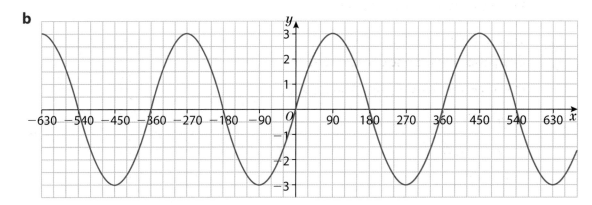

c

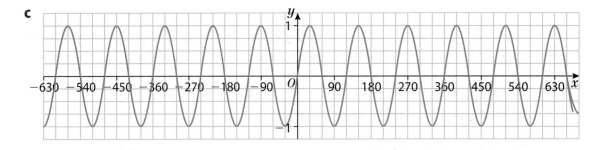

d

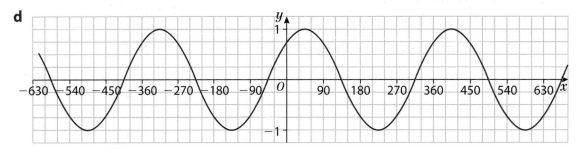

TASK 7: Transformations of functions

 Points to remember

⊙ A function $y = f(x)$ can be transformed in several ways.

⊙ $y = f(x) + a$ is a translation of a units in the y-direction.

⊙ $y = f(x + a)$ is a translation of $-a$ units in the x-direction.

⊙ $y = -f(x)$ is a reflection in the x-axis.

⊙ $y = f(-x)$ is a reflection in the y-axis.

⊙ $y = af(x)$ is a stretch of scale factor a in the y-direction.

⊙ $y = f(ax)$ is a stretch of scale factor $\frac{1}{a}$ in the x-direction.

You need some centimetre squared paper.

① The graph of $y = (x + 5)^2$ is translated 3 units in the negative direction of the x-axis.
Write the equation of the new graph.

② This is the graph of $y = f(x)$.
Copy the graph on squared paper.

On the same axes, sketch the graph of:

a $y = f(-x)$

b $y = -f(x)$

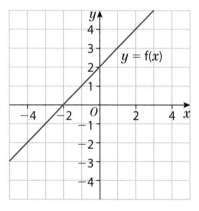

③ The graph of $y = x^2 + 2x$ is stretched by a scale factor of 3 parallel to the y-axis.
Write down the equation of the new graph.

④ The graph of $y = x^2$ is stretched by a scale factor of 3 parallel to the x-axis.
Write the equation of the new graph.

⑤ This is the graph of $y = f(x)$.
Copy the graph on squared paper.

On the same axes, sketch the graph of:

a $y = f(x + 2) - 1$

b $y = f(x - 2) + 1$

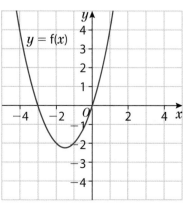

TASK 8: Loci

Points to remember

⊙ A **locus** is a set of points that obeys a given rule.

⊙ The set of points equidistant from two given points A and B is the perpendicular bisector of AB.

⊙ The set of points a fixed distance from point A is a circle, centre A.

⊙ The equation of a circle, centre (0, 0), radius r, is $x^2 + y^2 = r^2$.

⊙ The equation of a circle, centre (a, b), radius r, is $(x - a)^2 + (y - b)^2 = r^2$.

You need some graph paper.

(1) Sketch the locus of the point which moves so that it is equidistant from the given points.
Write the equation of each locus.

a (5, 0) and (0, 5)   **b** (−6, 0) and (0, 6)   **c** (−8, −2) and (−5, −5)

(2) Write the equations of these circles.

a centre (0, 0)
radius 1.5 units

b centre (1, 7)
radius 8 units

c centre (−5, −8)
radius 0.6 units

(3) **a** Draw on graph paper the circle with equation $x^2 + y^2 = 25$.

b Using the same axes, draw the straight line with equation $y = x + 1$.

c Use your graphs to estimate the solutions to the simultaneous equations
$x^2 + y^2 = 25$ and $y = x + 1$.

TASK 9: Solving problems

Points to remember

- Read through the problem and decide what mathematics to use.
- Define any variables you are going to use.
- Set up any expressions or equations using the information given.
- Solve the mathematical problem.
- Interpret the solution in the context of the original problem.
- Ask your own questions.

① The diagram shows a flag.
The flag is a square of side 56 cm.

The flag has a blue cross on a yellow background.
Each arm of the blue cross is the same width.

The blue area of the flag is equal to the
yellow area.

What is the width of an arm of the cross?
Give your answer to the nearest centimetre.

② The diagram shows a different flag.
The height of the flag is 60 cm and the
width 80 cm.

The width of the vertical stripe is twice
the depth of the horizontal stripe.
The area of the cross is half the area of the
whole flag.

What is the width of the vertical stripe?
Give your answer to the nearest centimetre.

Using and applying maths

TASK 1: The history of convex polyhedra

Points to remember

- People from many different cultures have contributed to what we now know about convex polyhedra, including mathematicians from Ancient Greece, Europe and America.

- There are five different Platonic solids, which are regular concave polyhedra with congruent vertices.

- There are eight different deltahedra and 13 different Archimedean solids.

- The Internet is a good source of information about maths and its history.

Did you know that...?

The Eden Project, Cornwall

A **geodesic dome** is a structure shaped like a part of a sphere. The design was invented by the American engineer **Richard Buckminster Fuller** in the 1940s. He had no formal technical training but taught himself. His ambition was to create a 'design science' that would be able to create the best solutions to problems with the minimal use of energy and materials.

'Buckey' Fuller became famous for creating the world's first geodesic dome in 1949. Its structure was a complex network of triangles that form a roughly spherical surface.

The Eden Project, in Cornwall, is housed in a series of geodesic domes.

1. Geodesic domes are elegant and sophisticated structures. Lightweight and strong, they make very efficient use of materials.

   Watch the video *Dome structures*. The video, which lasts 19 minutes, explains how to construct a model of a geodesic dome from paper and shows how to draw triangles with a compass and straight edge. The dome in the video was created by fitting four triangles onto each triangular face of an icosahedron. You can find it at:

   video.google.com/videoplay?docid=1183983212430151077

2. Continue your Internet research into complex polyhedra and write up notes ready to add to your PowerPoint presentation.

   Here are some websites that might help you.

   > **thesaurus.maths.org**
   > **plus.maths.org/issue27/features/mathart/index.html**
   > **en.wikipedia.org/wiki/Polyhedron**
   > **en.wikipedia.org/wiki/Archimedean_solids**
   > **mathworld.wolfram.com/Polyhedron.html**
   > **www-gap.dcs.st-and.ac.uk/~history/**

3. Read the article *Classifying solids using angle deficiency* by Warwick Evans. You can find this on the NRICH website at:

   nrich.maths.org/public/viewer.php?obj_id=1381

TASK 3: Algebraic proof

 Points to remember

- You can verify that an expression or formula is true or not true for a particular value by substituting that value into the expression or formula.
- Verifying that a statement is true for a particular value does not prove that it is always true.
- You can prove that a statement is true by using algebraic reasoning.

When a and b are integers, you can represent:

- three consecutive integers as a, $a + 1$, $a + 2$;
- an even number as $2a$ and two consecutive even numbers as $2a$ and $2a + 2$;
- an odd number as $2a + 1$ and two consecutive odd numbers as $2a - 1$ and $2a + 1$;
- a multiple of, say, 7 as $7a$;
- a two-digit number as $10a + b$.

To prove that a number is divisible by 7, or a multiple of 7, prove that 7 is a factor.

To prove that a number is even, prove that 2 is a factor.

(1) Prove that the sum of any two consecutive odd numbers is always a multiple of 4.

(2) Write down any three consecutive odd numbers.
Work out the square of the middle number.
Subtract the product of the first and last numbers.
Prove that the difference is always equal to 4.

(3) Think of a number, double it, subtract 4, multiply the result by 3, divide by 2, add 6, then divide by 3. Prove that the answer will always be equal to the number you started with.

(4) Choose any two-digit whole number.
Reverse the digits to form another two-digit number.
Add the two numbers.
Prove that the answer is always a multiple of 11.

(5) a and b are positive whole numbers, and:

$$\frac{a + c}{b + c} = \frac{1}{2}$$

Prove that c must also be a whole number.

TASK 4: Careers in mathematics

 Points to remember

⊙ The use of maths is widespread in everyday life, from sports, games and leisure pursuits, to driving and shopping, and practical tasks around the home or garden.

⊙ Many different occupations use maths in some way, sometimes in ways that are not immediately obvious.

1 In the lesson, you looked at the ways in which maths is used in everyday life and at work. You produced a presentation on three different occupations that make use of maths.

Car sales assistant

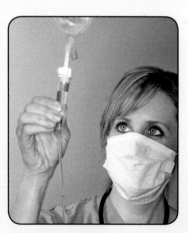
Nurse

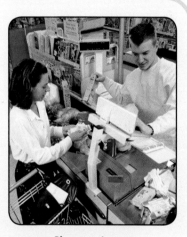
Shop assistant

Think about your presentation and how you went about it.

a Which occupations did you choose?
Explain how maths is used in each of them.

b Write down three occupations that other pupils chose.
Explain how maths is used in each of them.

c Which occupation might you choose as a career?
Describe some mathematics you have learned during this year and how it might be used in that occupation.

d How satisfied were you with the quality of your presentation?
Give your reasons.

e Describe two different ways in which you would improve your presentation if you were doing it again.

R 7.1 Revision unit 1

TASK 1: Percentages and ratios

Points to remember

- When a quantity is divided into two parts in the ratio $a : b$, the parts are $\dfrac{a}{a+b}$ and $\dfrac{b}{a+b}$ of the whole quantity.
- Calculate percentage increases and decreases, or reverse percentages, using the unitary method or decimal multipliers.
- Use the unitary method to solve problems involving direct or inverse proportion.

1. *1998 level 8*

   Look at the table.

	Birth rate per 1000 population	
	1961	1994
England	17.6	
Wales	17.0	12.2

   a In England, from 1961 to 1994, the birth rate fell by 26.1%.
   What was the birth rate in England in 1994? Show your working.

   b In Wales, the birth rate also fell.
   Calculate the percentage fall from 1961 to 1994. Show your working.

   c From 1961 to 1994, the birth rates in Scotland and Northern Ireland fell by the same amount. The percentage fall in Scotland was greater than in Northern Ireland.

   Which of the statements below is the true one?

   A In 1961, the birth rate in Scotland was higher than the birth rate in Northern Ireland.

   B In 1961, the birth rate in Scotland was the same as the birth rate in Northern Ireland.

   C In 1961, the birth rate in Scotland was lower than the birth rate in Northern Ireland.

   D From the information given, you cannot tell whether Scotland or Northern Ireland had the higher birth rate in 1961.

2 *1996 level 8*

Wendy is making a scale model of the Earth and the Moon for a museum.

She has found out the diameters of the Earth and the Moon, and the distance between them in centimetres.

Diameter of the Earth	1.28×10^9 cm
Diameter of the Moon	3.48×10^8 cm
Distance between Earth and Moon	3.89×10^{10} cm

a How many times bigger is the diameter of the Earth than the diameter of the Moon? Show your working.

b In Wendy's scale model the diameter of the Earth is 50 cm.
What should be the distance between the Earth and the Moon in Wendy's model? Show your working.

3 Using a scale of 1 cm : 50 000 000 km, a model of the Solar System will fit into a classroom.

How far from the model Sun would you place each model planet?
Give your answers in standard form.

	Planet	Distance from Sun (km)
a	Mercury	58 000 000
b	Venus	108 000 000
c	Earth	150 000 000
d	Mars	228 000 000
e	Jupiter	779 000 000
f	Saturn	1 427 000 000
g	Uranus	2 670 000 000
h	Neptune	4 496 000 000
i	Pluto	5 906 000 000

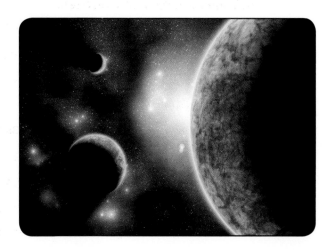

TASK 2: Expressions and equations

 Points to remember

- To work out the product of two expressions, multiply each term of the first expression by each term of the second expression.
- Factorising an expression is the opposite of expanding brackets. Work backwards to find the two brackets whose product is the expression.
- Two linear equations have a simultaneous solution when you can find a value for each variable that satisfies both equations.
- Two linear equations have no simultaneous solution when their graphs are parallel.

You need graph paper.

1 Which of these are correct?

    A $10(3a - 16) = 30a - 16$ **B** $(m + 7)(m - 3) = m^2 + 4m - 21$

    C $(d + 5)^2 = d^2 + 25$ **D** $(k - 3)(k + 3) = k^2 - 9$

2 Multiply out these expressions. Write your answers as simply as possible.

    a $(5x + 2)(6x + 3)$ **b** $(7x - 3)(4x + 3)$

    c $(8x - 5)(7x - 9)$ **d** $(4x - 3)^2$

3 **a** Draw graphs to solve these simultaneous equations.

$$4x + y = 5 \quad (1)$$
$$x - 2y = 8 \quad (2)$$

    b Use the method of elimination to solve these simultaneous equations.

$$3x + 2y = 19 \quad (1)$$
$$5x - 9y = 7 \quad (2)$$

    c Use the method of elimination to solve these simultaneous equations.

$$2x + 3y = 14 \quad (1)$$
$$3x + 2y = 6 \quad (2)$$

TASK 3: Formulae, functions and graphs

 Points to remember

⊙ A **formula** is a way of expressing a relationship using symbols.

⊙ When a formula starts $d = \ldots$, then d is called the subject of the formula.

⊙ You can rearrange a formula to make a different letter the subject, e.g.
$s = \dfrac{d}{t}$ and $t = \dfrac{d}{s}$.

⊙ The graph of $y = ax + b$ has gradient a and intercept on the y-axis at $(0, b)$.

⊙ Parallel lines have the same gradient.

⊙ Any line perpendicular to $y = ax + b$ has a gradient $-\dfrac{1}{a}$.

1   **a**   The subject of this formula is m.

$$m = 3(r + 2s)$$

Rearrange the formula to make s the subject.

    b   Rearrange the equation $p = 4(5q - 3r)$ to make r the subject.

2   The formula for the volume, V, of a cone is $V = \frac{1}{3}\pi r^2 h$.
r is the radius of the circular base and h is the perpendicular height.

Use $\pi \approx 3.14$.

    a   Find V when $r = 5\,\text{cm}$ and $h = 9\,\text{cm}$.

    b   Find h when $V = 65.94\,\text{cm}^3$ and $r = 3\,\text{cm}$.

    c   Find r when $V = 376.8\,\text{cm}^3$ and $h = 10\,\text{cm}$.

3   The red line on the right is line L.

    a   What is the equation of L?

    b   What is the equation of the line through $(0, 1)$ parallel to L?

    c   What is the equation of the line through $(-1, 1)$ parallel to L?

    d   What is the equation of the line through $(0, 6)$ perpendicular to L?

    e   What is the equation of the line through $(2, 1)$ perpendicular to L?

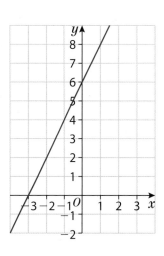

TASK 4: Geometrical reasoning

 Points to remember

⊙ Corresponding sides of **similar shapes** are in the same ratio.
⊙ Triangles are **congruent** if they satisfy SSS, SAS, ASA or RHS.
⊙ In a circle, the angle between a tangent and chord is a right angle.
⊙ The angle at the centre of a circle is twice the angle at the circumference.
⊙ The angle in a semicircle is a right angle.
⊙ Angles in the same segment are equal.
⊙ Opposite angles of a cyclic quadrilateral sum to 180°.

① *2007 level 8*

AC is the diameter of a circle and B is a point on the circumference of the circle.

What is the size of angle x?

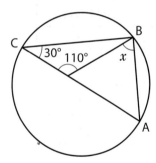

Not drawn accurately

② *GCSE 2540 November 2008*

In the diagram, AB = BC = CD = DA.

Prove that triangle ADB is congruent to triangle CDB.

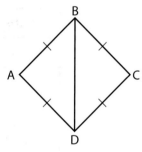

Not drawn accurately

③ *GCSE 2540 June 2008*

In the diagram, A, B, C and D are points on the circumference of a circle, centre O.

Angle BAD = 70°.
Angle BOD = x°.
Angle BCD = y°.

a Work out the value of x.
Give a reason for your answer.

b Work out the value of y.
Give a reason for your answer.

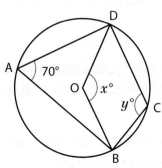

Not drawn accurately

TASK 5: Probability

Points to remember

- Mutually exclusive outcomes cannot occur at the same time. If events are mutually exclusive, the probability of **A** or **B** occurring is P(**A**) + P(**B**).

- Two events are independent if the outcomes of one event do not affect the outcomes of the other. For independent events, the probability of **A** and **B** occurring is P(**A**) × P(**B**).

- Tree diagrams are used to calculate probabilities. They are particularly useful when events are not equally likely or when they are not independent.

1 *2002 level 7*

A box contains cards with one question on each card. There are 4 categories of questions. Each category has some easy and some difficult questions.

The table shows the probability of selecting a card at random from the box.

Category	Easy	Difficult
Music	0.2	0.15
Sport	0.2	0.1
History	0.1	0.05
Nature	0.15	0.05

a I am going to take one card at random from the box. What is the probability that it will be:

i a history question?   **ii** an easy question?

b There are 40 cards in the box. How many of these are music questions?

2 *GCSE 1387 November 2006*

The probability that any piece of buttered toast will land buttered side down when it is dropped is 0.62.

Two pieces of buttered toast are to be dropped, one after the other.

Calculate the probability that exactly one piece of buttered toast will land buttered side down.

(3) *1995 level 8*

This dice with four faces has one blue, one green, one red and one yellow face.

Five pupils did an experiment to investigate whether the dice was biased or not.

The pupils collected all their data together.

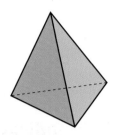

Number of throws	Face landed on			
	Red	Blue	Green	Yellow
520	179	186	75	80

a Consider the data.
Write down whether you think the dice is biased or unbiased, and explain your answer.

b From the data work out the probability of the dice landing on the blue face.

c From the data work out the probability of the dice landing on the green face.

d A pupil throws the dice twice. Work out the probability that the dice first lands on the blue face and then on the green face. Show your working.

(4) *GCSE 1387 November 2004*

In a game of chess, you can win, draw or lose.

Gary plays two games of chess against Mijan.
The probability that Gary will win any game against Mijan is 0.55.
The probability that Gary will draw any game against Mijan is 0.3.

a Work out the probability that Gary will win exactly one of the two games against Mijan.

In a game of chess, you score

1 point for a win,

0.5 points for a draw,

0 points for a loss.

b Work out the probability that after two games, Gary's total score will be the same as Mijan's total score.

Revision unit 2

TASK 1: Indices and standard form

> **Points to remember**
>
> ⊙ $\sqrt[n]{a}$ or $a^{1/n}$ means the nth root of a.
>
> ⊙ $a^m \times a^n = a^{m+n}$, $a^m \div a^n = a^{m-n}$ and $(a^m)^n = a^{m \times n}$,
> for positive or negative integer or fractional values of m and n.
>
> ⊙ A number in standard form is of the form $A \times 10^n$, where $1 \leqslant A < 10$ and
> n is an integer.
>
> ⊙ Standard form is a useful way of writing very large or very small numbers.
>
> ⊙ Answers to calculations involving numbers in standard form are usually
> given to 3 significant figures.

1 *1998 level 8*

   a Which of these statements is true?

     A 4×10^3 is a larger number than 4^3.

     B 4×10^3 is the same size as 4^3.

     C 4×10^3 is a smaller number than 4^3.

     Explain your answer.

   b One of the numbers below has the same value as 3.6×10^4.
     Which number is it?

     36^3 36^4 $(3.6 \times 10)^4$ 0.36×10^3 0.36×10^5

   c One of the numbers below has the same value as 2.5×10^{-3}.
     Which number is it?

     25×10^{-4} 2.5×10^3 -2.5×10^3 $0.000\,25$ 2500

   d $(2 \times 10^2) \times (2 \times 10^2)$ can be written simply as 4×10^4.
     Write these values as simply as possible:

     i $(3 \times 10^2) \times (2 \times 10^{-2})$ **ii** $\dfrac{6 \times 10^3}{2 \times 10^4}$

2 *2001 level 8*

$\frac{1}{2500}$ is equal to 0.0004.

    a Write 0.0004 in standard form.   **b** Write $\frac{1}{25\,000}$ in standard form.

    c Work out $\frac{1}{2500} + \frac{1}{25\,000}$. Show your working, and write your answer in standard form.

3 Mercury is 3.6×10^7 miles from the Sun. It takes 88 days to go round the Sun. Assuming that its orbit is a circle, find its average speed in miles per hour.

4 The volume of a sphere is $\frac{4}{3}\pi r^3$, where r is the radius.
A single-celled protozoa has a volume of about $0.004\,\text{mm}^3$.
Assuming that it is spherical in shape, write its diameter in metres.

TASK 2: Equations and inequalities

Points to remember

⊙ Solve linear equations by using inverse operations.

⊙ When you draw graphs of linear inequalities, shade the unwanted regions.

⊙ Some quadratic equations can be solved by factorising.

⊙ When you cannot find factors of a quadratic equation, use the formula $x = \dfrac{-b \pm \sqrt{b^2 - 4ac}}{2a}$ to find solutions.

1 Solve these linear equations.

    a $9(2x + 5) - 4(3x + 1) = 65$ **b** $3(7x + 4) - 5(2x - 6) = 32x$

    c $\dfrac{3x}{2} + \dfrac{5x}{3} = 2x + 7$ **d** $\dfrac{5}{2x} + \dfrac{4}{5x} = 0.3$

2 Shozna has saved £30 to spend on music downloads.
Tracks cost £1.20 a download from website A and 90p from website B.
x is the number of downloads from site A and y is the number of downloads from site B.

    a Explain why $120x + 90y \leqslant 3000$.

    b Explain why $x \geqslant 0$ and $y \geqslant 0$.

    c Sketch a graph to show the region that satisfies all three inequalities.

3 Use factorisation to solve these quadratic equations.
Check your answers by substituting each value for x back into the original equation.

a $x^2 - 12x + 35 = 0$ **b** $x^2 - 4x - 32 = 0$

4 Use the quadratic formula to solve these equations.
Give your answers to three significant figures.

a $x^2 - 9x - 5 = 0$ **b** $x^2 + 6x - 2 = 0$

TASK 3: Functions and graphs

Did you know that…?

A graphics calculator can help you to solve equations.

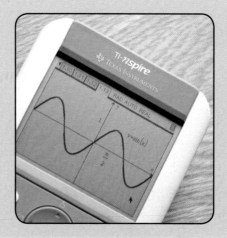

Points to remember

⊙ A polynomial equation is of the form $y = ax^n + bx^{n-1} + cx^{n-2} + \ldots$, where n is a positive integer.

⊙ A reciprocal equation is of the form $y = \dfrac{a}{bx}$.

⊙ An exponential equation is of the form $y = a^x$.

⊙ A trigonometric equation is of the form
$y = a \sin bx$, $y = a \cos bx$ or $y = a \tan bx$

⊙ A function $f(x)$ can be transformed as follows:
  - $f(x) + a$ is a translation of a units in the y-direction;
  - $f(x + a)$ is a translation of $-a$ units in the x-direction;
  - $af(x)$ is a stretch with scale factor a in the y-direction;
  - $f(ax)$ is a stretch with scale factor $\dfrac{1}{a}$ in the x-direction;
  - $-f(x)$ is a reflection in the x-axis;
  - $f(-x)$ is a reflection in the y-axis.

1. Match each function to one of the graphs **A** to **F**.

a $f(x) = 2^x - 1$

b $f(x) = \dfrac{3}{x}$

c $f(x) = x^2 + 0.5$

d $f(x) = -x^3 + 3x^2 - 2$

e $f(x) = 2 \sin x$

f $f(x) = \cos 6x$

A

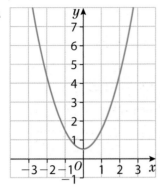

B

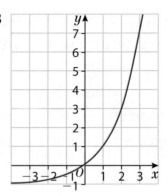

C

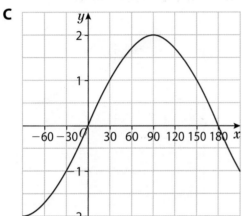

D

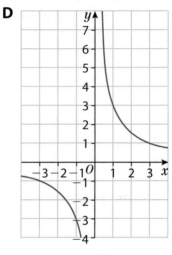

E

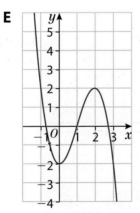

F

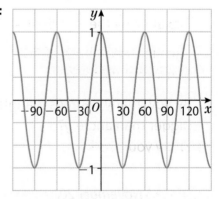

2. In each question, g(x) is a transformation of f(x). Describe the transformation.

a $f(x) = -x^2 + 5$
   $g(x) = x^2 - 5$

b $f(x) = 2x + 1$
   $g(x) = 2x - 4$

c $f(x) = x^2$
   $g(x) = x^2 - 2x + 1$

d $f(x) = 3^x$
   $g(x) = 3^{-x}$

e $f(x) = \cos x$
   $g(x) = \cos 8x$

f $f(x) = \cos x$
   $g(x) = 6 \cos x$

TASK 4: Pythagoras' theorem and trigonometry

Points to remember

⊙ If you know two sides of a right-angled triangle:
  – use Pythagoras' theorem to work out the length of the third side;
  – use trigonometric ratios to find angles.

⊙ If you know one acute angle and one side of a right-angled triangle:
  – use trigonometric ratios to find the lengths of the other sides.

⊙ Use the formula for the area of a circle to find areas of sectors of circles.

You can use **trigonometric ratios** to work out the lengths of sides and the sizes of angles in right-angled triangles.

$$\sin x = \frac{\text{opposite}}{\text{hypotenuse}}$$

$$\cos x = \frac{\text{adjacent}}{\text{hypotenuse}}$$

$$\tan x = \frac{\text{opposite}}{\text{adjacent}}$$

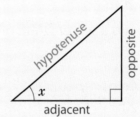

You need squared paper, a ruler and a pencil.

 1 *2000 level 8*

ABC and ACD are both right-angled triangles.

a Explain why the length of AC is 10 cm.

b Calculate the length of AD.
Show your working.

c By how many degrees is angle x bigger than angle y?
Show your working.

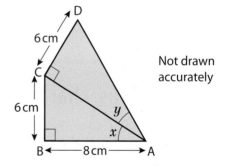

Not drawn accurately

2 *GCSE 1385 November 2002*

ABD and DBC are two right-angled triangles.

AB = 9 m
Angle ABD = 35°
Angle DBC = 50°

Calculate the length of DC.
Give your answer correct to 3 significant figures.

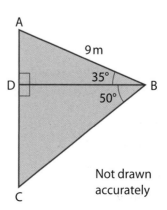

Not drawn accurately

3 *GCSE 1387 June 2004*

The diagram represents a prism.
AEFD is a rectangle.
ABCD is a square.
EB and FC are perpendicular to plane ABCD.

AB = 60 cm
AD = 60 cm
Angle ABE = 90°
Angle BAE = 30°

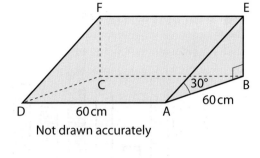

Not drawn accurately

Calculate the size of the angle that the line DE makes with the plane ABCD.
Give your answer correct to 1 decimal place.

4 *GCSE 1387 June 2006*

The diagram shows a sector OABC of a circle with centre O.

OA = OC = 10.4 cm
Angle AOC = 120°

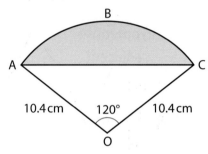

Not drawn accurately

a Calculate the length of the arc ABC of the sector.
   Give your answer correct to 3 significant figures.

b Calculate the area of the shaded segment ABC.
   Give your answer correct to 3 significant figures.

TASK 5: Graphs, charts and statistics

⊙ Points to remember

⊙ A cumulative frequency graph can be used to find the median and the interquartile range.

⊙ Graphs and statistics can be used to compare distributions.

You need graph paper.

1 *2005 level 7*

Here are four charts showing the average amount of milk produced by some cow breeds.

Chart 1

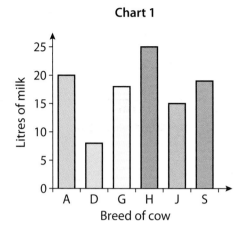

Chart 2

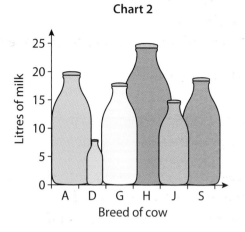

Chart 3

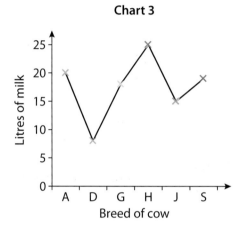

Chart 4

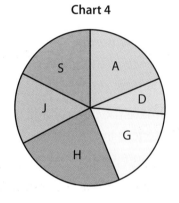

Key: A: Ayrshire   D: Dexter   G: Guernsey   H: Holstein   J: Jersey   S: Shorthorn

Only one of these charts is a good way of showing the data.
For each of the other three charts, explain why the type of chart is not a good way of showing the data.

2 *2004 level 7*

Altogether, I have 10 bags of sweets.
The mean number of sweets in a bag is 41.

The table shows how many sweets there are in
9 of the bags.

No. of sweets in a bag	39	40	41	42	43	44
Frequency	3	2	1	1	0	2

Calculate how many sweets there are in the 10th bag. Show your working.

3 *2001 level 8*

The first *Thomas the Tank Engine* stories were written in 1945. In the 1980s, the stories were rewritten.

The cumulative frequency graph shows the numbers of words per sentence for one of the stories.

There are 58 sentences in the old version. There are 68 sentences in the new version.

a Estimate the median number of words per sentence in the old version and in the new version.

b What can you tell from the data about the number of words per sentence in the old version and in the new version?

c Estimate the percentage of sentences in the old version that had more than 12 words per sentence. Show your working.

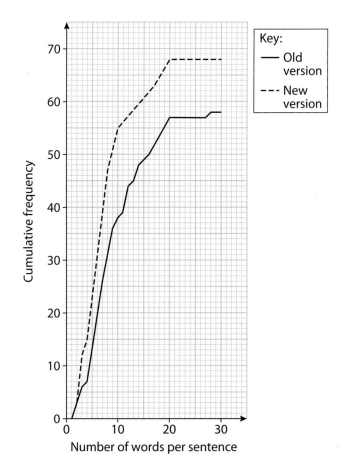

Key:
— Old version
--- New version

4 80 caterpillars were divided into 2 groups.

Group A were reared indoors.
Group B were reared outdoors.

After a period of time the lengths of the caterpillars were measured.

The lengths were used to draw two cumulative frequency graphs.

	Group A	Group B
Shortest caterpillar (cm)	1.6	0.3
Longest caterpillar (cm)	4.4	3.8

a Use the information provided in the table and the cumulative frequency graphs to draw box plots of the lengths of the caterpillars in group A and the lengths of the caterpillars in group B.

b Compare the lengths of the caterpillars in the two groups.

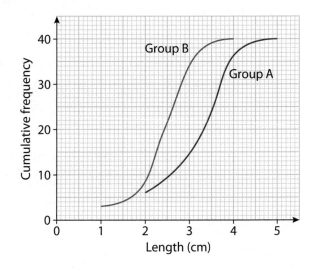